oliver + s

little things to sew

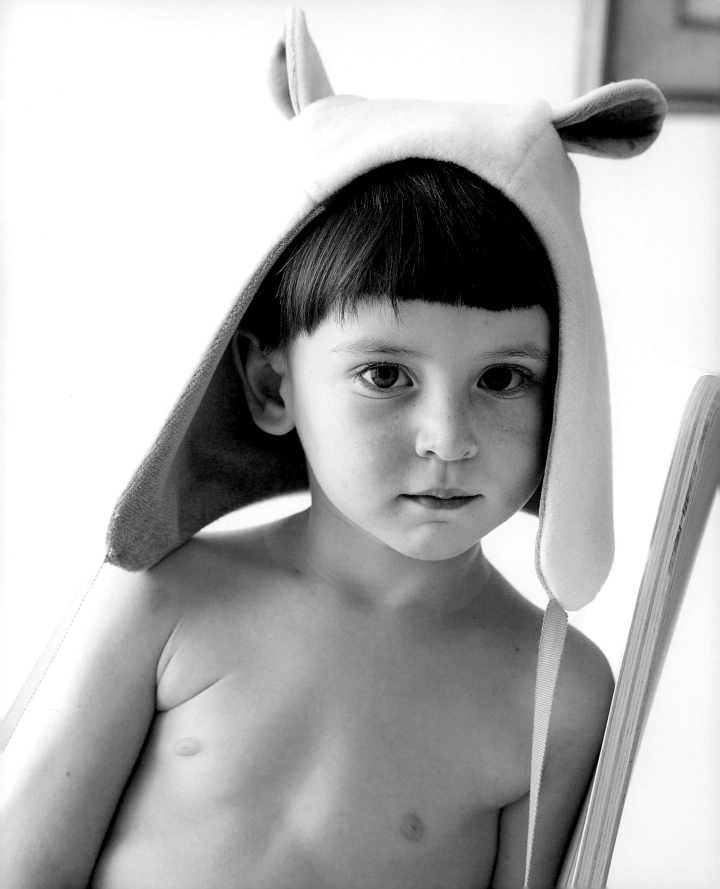

oliver + s

little things
to sew

20 CLASSIC ACCESSORIES AND TOYS FOR CHILDREN

liesl gibson

photographs by laurie frankel
paper doll illustrations by dan andreasen

STC CRAFT | A MELANIE FALICK BOOK
STEWART, TABORI & CHANG
NEW YORK

Published in 2011 by Stewart, Tabori & Chang
An imprint of ABRAMS

Library of Congress Cataloging-in-Publication Data

Gibson, Liesl.
Oliver + S little things to sew : 20 classic accessories and toys for children / Liesl Gibson ;
photographs by Laurie Frankel ; paper doll illustrations by Dan Andreasen.
p. cm.
ISBN 978-1-58479-910-8 (alk. paper)
1. Dress accessories. 2. Children's clothing. 3. Soft toy making. I. Title.
TT635.G52 2011
646.4'06--dc22
                              2010014204

Editor: Melanie Falick
Technical Editor: Christine Timmons
Designer: Brooke Reynolds for inchmark
Production Manager: Tina Cameron

The text of this book was composed in Nobel.

Printed and bound in China.

10   9   8   7   6   5   4

THE ART OF BOOKS SINCE 1949

115 West 18th Street
New York, NY 10011
www.abramsbooks.com

contents

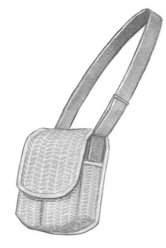

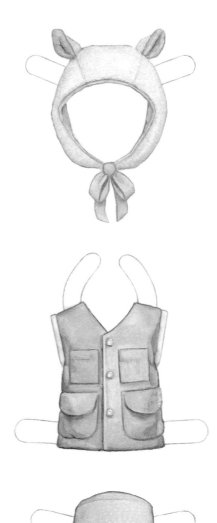

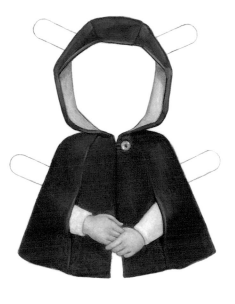

introduction

I like little. I always have. But having a child has helped me to appreciate little things in new ways.

While I was growing up, I had a set of small books that I adored. Each book told a tiny tale and was illustrated with exquisite pictures. I was able to locate the same books for my daughter (whose nickname is S), and she loves them as much as I did for their stories, illustrations, and diminutive size. Her favorite toys are always the little things (dolls, pencils, books) that fit easily into small hands and small pockets.

After S was born, I took a leave from my job as a clothing designer to be with her. I wanted to sew for her, but because I couldn't find patterns I liked, I designed and drafted my own. I was making clothing with contemporary styling and a classic feel that featured unique and interesting dressmaking details.

A friend encouraged me to publish the patterns, and my husband helped me research the market and write a business plan. Before long I was launching Oliver + S with a first line featuring four patterns in two size ranges. We've grown steadily since, thanks to the support and feedback we receive from our customers. We've developed a reputation for great dressmaking details, excellent and thorough instructions, and an appealing style.

In *Oliver + S Little Things to Sew* I apply the same approach I take with garment patterns to accessories and toys. The projects here came about in a variety of ways. The Tutu (page 14), Bias-Trimmed Apron (page 36), and Art Smock (page 60) are all new takes on classic childhood items. I made each unique by putting my own spin on it. The Tutu, for example, is constructed like a classic apron that fastens around the waist with a ribbon, rather than with the usual elastic waistband.

I developed other projects by watching how my daughter and her friends explore and respond to the little things around them. The Bear Carrier (page 104) came about because S wanted to carry her favorite stuffed animal on her chest in the same way that parents carry newborns in baby carriers. Similarly, watching S and her friends gather stones, twigs, and other little treasures inspired me to design the Explorer Vest (page 98) with lots of pockets.

Still other projects are my take on useful, everyday items. For example, the Messy Kid Bib (page 70) is specially designed to catch spills before they hit the child's lap.

Art Smock (see page 60)

No-Tie Scarf (see page 20)

And the Messenger Bag (page 24) is customizable to your taste (you can select any fabric or print you want) and can be made in two sizes, depending on the size of the user.

As with the Oliver + S garment patterns, each project in this book is rated by difficulty using a one-to-four scissors system.

BEGINNER: Suitable for someone who has either taken a first-level sewing class or has learned to sew from a book or video. Assumes familiarity with a sewing machine; understanding of how to sew a seam, thread the machine, etc.; and successful completion of a few small projects.

ADVANCED BEGINNER: Suitable for someone who has sewn from a pattern before or has taken a few classes and completed several projects.

INTERMEDIATE: For the experienced sewer who has made a wider variety of items and feels comfortable with a new challenge.

ADVANCED: For a very experienced sewer who can handle any challenge.

Many of our customers tell us that, thanks to our detailed instructions, sewing from our patterns feels like taking a class. Oftentimes, people are amazed to realize that they can successfully complete projects that they initially thought might be too hard for them. I encourage you to use our rating system as a guide

but not to shy away from a project that requires learning a new skill because everything you need to know is right there in the instructions.

If you find you have questions while sewing any of the projects in this book, or if you want to comment on them, please visit the Discussion Forums section of our website: www.oliverands.com.

As you sew your way through the projects in this book, I hope your appreciation of little things will grow. Enjoy the little details I've included in these projects. Improve your technique by following the little lessons the instructions provide. And, most of all, take more than a little pleasure in the process of creating unique items that will be enjoyed by the little people in your life.

Happy sewing!

Liesl

mittens

Many children resist wearing mittens because they don't like the way they feel against their skin and the way they restrict their hand movement. Keeping those concerns in mind, I designed these mittens to be sewn in a microfiber fleece or a soft wool felt, both of which feel good next to the skin. The construction method (using a seam that crosses the palm and forms the thumb) creates extra room inside so that little hands can move around easily.

ASSEMBLE THE MITTEN

1. With right sides together, align and pin one mitten front top and front bottom together at the curved thumb. Join the pair with a ¼" seam, backstitching at both ends of the seam.

2. Press the thumb and seam allowances toward the curved finger edge of the front top piece, forming a crease at the base of the thumb.

3. With right sides together, align and pin the mitten front to the mitten back. Stitch the edge closest to the thumb, starting at the top edge and ending 3"-4" down, backstitching or lockstitching at the beginning and end of your stitching to secure it.

4. Open the mitten, and lay it right side up. Using a water-soluble fabric-marking pen or chalk, draw a line 1" below the mitten's upper (wrist) edge. Then also draw a vertical line ¼" from each outside edge of the mitten. You'll use these drawn lines to position the casing in the next step.

5. Fold and press the long, raw edges of the casing to the wrong side, so they meet at the center. Then pin the casing, right side up, so its upper long edge meets the 1" line you drew in Step 4. Trim the casing's short ends to be about ½" longer than the ¼"-edge lines that you also drew in Step 4, and then fold and press these short edges to the wrong side before pinning them to the mitten, so the folded edges meet the ¼"-edge lines.

6. Edgestitch the long sides of the casing to the mitten, staying as close to the edges as you can comfortably stitch, and backstitching or lockstitching at the beginning and end of the casing to secure your stitches. Leave the short ends of the casing unstitched.

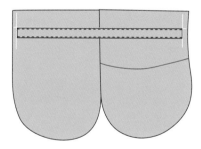

7. With right sides together, align and pin the two halves of the mitten again; and finish stitching the perimeter with a ¼" seam. Take care as you reach the casing ends not to stitch over the casing, but instead stitch just off to the side of the casing's ends.

1. Use a shortened zigzag stitch to satin-stitch the top of the mitten and finish its raw edge. You could also use a decorative stitch if you prefer, instead of the zigzag stitch.

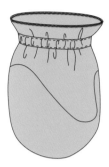

2. Pin a safety pin to the end of a length of elastic, and use the safety pin to feed the elastic through the casing. You can use the following approximate elastic lengths as a guideline, but keep in mind that different qualities of elastic have varying amounts of stretch, so adjust as necessary: extra-small, 6 ½"; small, 7"; medium, 7 ½"; large, 8".

Adjust the length of the elastic as desired, and attach the two ends to each other with a few secure hand stitches before blindstitching the casing openings together by hand to finish the mitten.

tutu

Little girls love this classic-style tutu because of the way the tulle floats up and around as they twirl. This tutu can be made with one color of tulle or several, which provides an interesting visual effect when worn. It is constructed like a wide apron using the child's waist size as a guide, which makes it reversible and adjustable, assuring a good fit. When the ribbon waistband is tied around the child's waist, the layers of tulle overlap in the back, making the opening nearly invisible. Most tulle is more than 100" wide when it's laid flat, so it helps to have a lot of space and a friend to assist you when you are folding and positioning the layers at the start.

SKILLS NEEDED
Edgestitching, Gathering

FINISHED SIZE
Any size you like—our sample (17" long with 20" waist) fits size 3-5

MATERIALS
1-2 yds. each of five different colors of tulle (see instructions for gauging specific yardage)

3 yds. of 1"- or 1 ½"-wide ribbon (grosgrain works well)

Coordinating thread

Heavy thread (like upholstery thread), for gathering

Rotary cutter and cutting mat

Chalk or water-soluble fabric-marking pen

Seam sealant or fabric glue (optional)

1. Estimate the skirt length for your tutu (ours measured 17" from waist to hem), and double that measurement to get the cut length of tulle needed (for a 17" tutu, the cut length was 34"). Then purchase five pieces of tulle cut to the length of your doubled measurement. For our tutu, we bought 1 yard each of peach, dark pink, and rust tulle, and 2 yards of yellow tulle (since the yellow was especially light in color, two layers helped it show up better against the brighter colors).

1. Measure the child's waist, and cut a piece of ribbon to that measurement. The finished tutu's actual waistband will be 1" smaller than the child's waist measurement to leave room for tying the bow and to keep the tutu from falling down when worn. Mark the cut ribbon with chalk or a pin placed ½" from each end. We'll call this ribbon the short ribbon and the remaining ribbon (which you can set aside temporarily) the long ribbon.

2. Fold the short ribbon in half, and mark the center with a pin or chalk. Fold the ribbon in half again to find its quarter measurements, and likewise mark each of those quadrants with a pin or chalk. Your marked ribbon will be divided into equal quadrants, with a ½" seam allowance at each end.

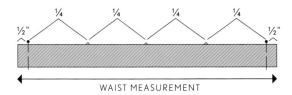

WAIST MEASUREMENT

1. Cut the pieces of tulle to the doubled-length measurement you determined above, and use the tulle's full width (tulle often measures 108" wide).

> **HINT:** A rotary cutter and cutting mat are really helpful for this step, since you can fold the fabric width several times and cut the entire piece of folded tulle in just one short pass.

2. Clear a large space on the floor on which to prepare the cut lengths of tulle. Have a friend help you open up the first piece of tulle to its full width, then fold it in half lengthwise so that it's doubled, with the fold at the top. Lay the first folded layer flat.

3. Open the second piece of tulle, fold it the same way, and lay it on top of the first folded layer, aligning the folded edges and pinning them every 5" or 6" to keep the layers aligned.

4. Similarly fold and layer the third piece on top of the other two pieces, re-pinning the folded edges of all three layers. Continue this way until you've laid out and pinned all five pieces together at the top folded edge. (For the tutus in the photograph, we layered our tulle with yellow on the top followed by a second layer of yellow and then rust, peach, and dark pink below.)

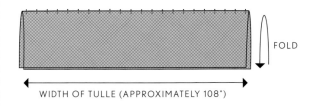

FOLD

WIDTH OF TULLE (APPROXIMATELY 108")

1. With heavy thread in the bobbin, machine-baste all the layers of tulle together about ⅝" from the folded and pinned edge, leaving thread tails several inches long at the beginning and end of your basting. Stitch a second row of basting stitches ⅛" above the first row, and a third row of basting ⅛" above the second row (⅜" from the top folded edge), again leaving long thread tails at the beginning and end of each basting row.

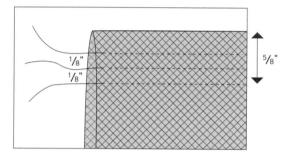

2. Fold the layers of tulle in half widthwise, and use a safety pin to mark the center of the width. Fold each half in half again to mark each quadrant with a safety pin.

ATTACH THE RIBBONS

1. Leaving the first and last ½" of the short ribbon free, start pinning the ribbon to one side of the tulle at each quadrant marking, matching the ribbon's bottom edge to the bottom row of basting stitches, so the ribbon covers all the stitches. Then pull on the heavy bobbin threads of the gathering stitches to gather the tulle, until the tulle's width matches the ribbon's length. Finish pinning the gathered tulle to the ribbon, adjusting the gathers evenly across the ribbon's length.

2. Edgestitch or zigzag-stitch the ribbon to the tulle near the ribbon's bottom edge (positioning the tutu so that the ribbon is on top for this stitching will yield the best-looking results).

> **HINT:** I prefer a zigzag stitch because it helps flatten the multiple layers of tulle and prevents the tulle from detaching from the ribbon when you trim it in the next step.

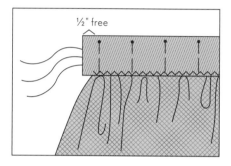

3. Carefully trim the excess tulle and basting stitches above the stitching at the ribbon's bottom edge to eliminate excess bulk from the ribbon waistband. Then fold and pin the ½" seam allowances at the ends of the ribbon over the edges of the tulle.

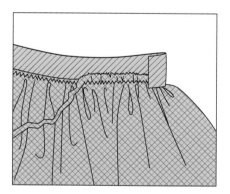

4. Find the center of the long ribbon (the ribbon you set aside), and pin it to the center of the waistband ribbon on the tutu's wrong side, sandwiching the tulle's cut edge between the two ribbons. Pin the full length of the short ribbon to the long ribbon, matching the edges and tucking the short ribbon's folded ends between the layers.

5. Edgestitch the short ribbon to the long ribbon, starting at the top edge of the ribbons and pivoting at the corners of the short ribbon to stitch a rectangle (you'll restitch the bottom of the ribbon in this step). This will finish the waistband cleanly and prevent the scratchy ends of the tulle from irritating delicate skin.

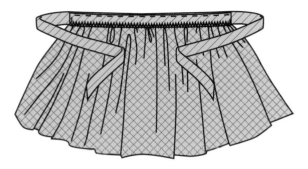

FINISH THE TUTU

1. Trim the ends of the long ribbon at a 45-degree angle. If you want, apply a little seam sealant or fabric glue to the ribbon's cut ends to prevent fraying.

2. I like the slightly varied lengths of the tulle to show at the hem, so I prefer not to trim the hem when the tutu is finished. However, if the tutu is too long, you can trim the tulle to your desired length. Measure from the top of the waistband, and mark the length you want with pins or a water-soluble fabric-marking pen. Then carefully cut each layer individually, so each layer will be a little different from the next.

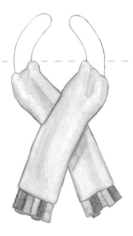

no-tie scarf

I've always admired knitted scarves where one end slides through an opening on the other side. Scarves like this are especially functional for kids because they don't need to be tied, and they stay wrapped warmly around little necks on cold days. I created a knitting pattern for one a few years ago, and since then I've made several.

I figured there had to be a way to make the same type of scarf from a woven fabric, and here it is. This is an easy-to-sew project with lots of room for creative embellishment. For example, you could use rickrack or fabric scraps for the fringe or appliqué shapes onto the scarf for additional flair.

FINISHED SIZES

Small, fits up to size 3, 34" x 5" (*medium*, sizes 4-6, 37" x 5"; *large*, size 7 and up, 40" x 5")

MATERIALS

NOTE: In dimensions throughout, length precedes width.

FABRIC A: ¼ yd. of 44"-wide wool coating, wool melton or tweed, cashmere, fine-wale corduroy, cotton flannel, velveteen*, or micro-fleece, for front

FABRIC B: ¼ yd. of 44"-wide flannel or other mid- to light-weight, soft cotton, for back

FABRIC C: two 6" squares of lightweight fabric, for scarf loop

Scraps, about 4" x 8", of three or more fabrics, plus optional trims, for fringe

Coordinating thread

Pinking shears

Paper scissors

Tissue paper

Scarf pattern
(see Pattern Sheet 1; Pattern 2, two pieces: A-B)

*NOTE: Velveteen, or cotton velvet, is more difficult to work with than the other recommended fabrics for this project, so if this is a first sewing project for you, we suggest using one of the other fabrics mentioned.

ATTACH THE LOOP TO THE SCARF

1. Align and pin one of the two cut loop pieces to the Fabric A scarf front, with right sides together, matching the loop's raw edges with the scarf's notches. Stitch the sides together between the dots you transferred from the pattern, backstitching or lockstitching at the beginning and end of your stitches and stopping precisely at the dots.

2. Press the seam allowances open. Turn the scarf and loop right side out.

3. Repeat steps 1-2 with the second cut loop and the Fabric B scarf back.

JOIN THE SCARF FRONT AND BACK

1. Fold and press the short ends of the scarf front and back to the wrong side by ½". Fold the unstitched raw edges of the cut loop pieces to the right side, and pin them to keep them out of the way for the next steps.

2. Align and pin the scarf front and back together, with right sides together, carefully matching the dots you transferred from the pattern. Then stitch the scarf's long edges, starting at one dot and stitching to the end of the scarf and then repeating the process on each of the remaining edges. Backstitch or lockstitch precisely at the dots, being careful not to stitch the loop pieces in this step. This can be a bit fiddly, so take your time and adjust the fabric layers as you sew, if necessary.

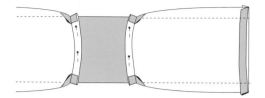

3. Unpin the loop's seam allowances, and start turning the scarf wrong side out through one end. Just as the loop pieces are about to disappear completely into the tube (all but the final seam allowances will already have disappeared from view), align and pin the seam allowances of the loop pieces on the scarf front and back, with right sides together. Stitch only the loop pieces together with a ½" seam, stitching all the way across from one dot to the other.

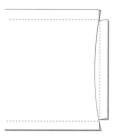

4. Turn the scarf right side out again, reversing what you had started. Then start turning the scarf wrong side out through the other end in order to stitch the loop's opposite seam allowances.

5. Turn the scarf right side out again, and press the seams to encourage the scarf to lie flat.

FINISH THE SCARF

1. Cut a rectangle, about 4" x 8", from each of your fabric scraps.

2. Fold each rectangle in half, with the right side out, so the long edges match. Then, using pinking shears, cut strips of folded fabric (these will be the scarf fringes) between ⅝" and 1" wide.

3. Using your paper scissors, cut a strip of tissue paper 4 ½" x 1". Start arranging the folded fringe pieces (with the folded edges out) next to each other on the tissue paper, leaving a little gap between the pieces to create a row of fringes that are slightly less than the width of the tissue paper strip. Lay a second row of scraps on top of the first row to cover the spaces in the first row.

4. When you're pleased with the arrangement, pin the fringes to the tissue paper, and baste it together with a ³⁄₈" seam. Then carefully tear away the tissue paper, leaving just the fringe.

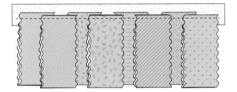

5. Slip the row of basted fringe into the opening at one end of the scarf so that the basting is hidden inside the scarf. Then stitch all the layers together using a decorative or zigzag stitch ¹⁄₈" from the end of the scarf.

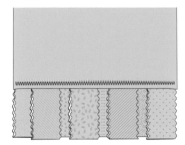

6. Repeat steps 2-5 to add fringe on the opposite end of the scarf. If you choose not to add the fringe, either hand-stitch the ends of the scarf closed with a blindstitch or use a decorative machine stitch to finish the ends (see Step 5 above).

messenger bag

I based this messenger bag on a favorite adult-sized bag that we have at home. Our bag has room to carry lunch, a water bottle, a laptop computer, a sketchbook, and a few other necessities, but it doesn't look bulky.

The bag in this photo is sized for children up to age five, but the pattern also includes a version for older children and adults (see photo on page 29). If you use the suggested strap adjuster hardware, the bag can grow with the child or be used by people of different sizes.

SKILLS NEEDED

Sewing curved seam, Applying bias binding

FINISHED SIZES

Small, 7½" x 10" x 2¾", fits up to 5 yrs. (*large*, 10" x 13" x 3½", fits 6 yrs. to adult)

MATERIALS

NOTE: In cutting dimensions throughout, length precedes width.

FABRIC A: ½ yd. (1 yd.) of 44"-wide, medium-weight fabric like home-dec fabric, canvas, or denim, for outside of bag (see note on next page)

FABRIC B: ½ yd. (1 yd.) of 44"-wide, light- to medium-weight fabric like quilting cotton, for lining

FABRIC C: ½ yd. (½ yd.) of 44"-wide, medium-weight fabric like home-dec fabric, denim, or lightweight canvas, for straps

½ yd. (1 yd.) of 44"-wide canvas, for backing Fabric A (optional)

4 yds. (4½ yds.) of ½"-wide homemade bias binding (see page 126) or 2 packages of ½"-wide, double-folded, ready-made bias binding

Two 1½"-wide (2"-wide) strap adjusters (see Resources on page 134)

Snaps, for pocket closures (optional)

Coordinating thread

Water-soluble fabric-marking pen or chalk

Walking foot (recommended)

Messenger Bag pattern (see Pattern Sheet 2; Pattern 6; nine pieces: A-I) and cutting diagram on page 124; plus one 39" x 6" (43" x 8") piece from Fabric C and one 6" x 6" (9" x 8") piece; no pattern piece or cutting layout provided for straps)

Because the outside fabric for this bag needs body to maintain the bag's structure, we recommend either using a medium-weight (10-oz.) canvas or backing a lightweight fabric with a layer of light-weight (8-oz.) canvas or heavy interfacing, but be careful not to choose fabrics that are too thick or bulky. If you're using quilting-weight cotton, you can either baste the fabric to the canvas around the outside edges with a ¼" seam or pin the layers together temporarily while you sew. Basting takes more time but is more effective than pinning to keep the layers from shifting during construction. Once you've basted or pinned the two layers together, you can treat them as one fabric. We'll refer to the two layers as the outside fabric in the cutting and sewing instructions.

NOTE: Because the seams can get bulky, you may find it helpful to use a walking foot for this project. Use a strong needle in your machine.

CUT AND MAKE THE STRAPS

1. From Fabric C, cut a 6" square (9" x 8" square) for the bag's short strap and a 39" x 6" (43" x 8") piece for its long strap. Fold the long strap in half lengthwise, with wrong sides together, and press the crease to create a center fold line.

2. Open the strap, and lay it flat and wrong side up. Fold each long raw edge in toward the center crease, and press the folds.

3. Fold the strap in half again along the center crease, and press it, enclosing the raw edges in the fold. The strap is now folded into four fabric thicknesses.

4. Finish the strap by edgestitching it along the open edge and again along the opposite folded edge.

5. Repeat steps 1 – 4 to make the short strap.

ASSEMBLE THE FRONT BAG

1. Using the notches as a guide, draw a line down the center of the front pocket and the front panel on the fabric's right side with a water-soluble fabric-marking pen or chalk. You'll use these lines as a pinning and stitching guide shortly.

2. Align and pin the front pocket and front pocket lining, with wrong sides together, and baste the edges with a ¼" seam if you want. Apply bias binding to the pocket's straight top edge (see "Working with bias binding" on page 126 for details).

3. Pin the front pocket to the front panel along the center-front lines that you drew in Step 1 above, matching the bottom raw edges. Topstitch the center-front line, starting at the front panel's top edge, stitching through all the layers of the pocket and front panel, and backstitching at the beginning and end of the seam to secure your stitches.

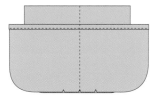

4. Fold the front pocket in half, with right sides together, and fold the front panel in half in the opposite direction so that the two pieces touch only at the seam line. Using a water-soluble fabric-marking pen or chalk, draw a line on the pocket lining 1½" (2") to the right of the seam line (use the notches and lines on the pattern piece to help you locate the position of the line). Baste the layers of the pocket together along this line.

5. Open the front panel, and lay it flat. Then press the front pocket's basted seam line to the center-front stitching from Step 3 to form an inverted pleat for the front pockets. Baste all the layers together around the outside edges of the front panel to keep the resulting pleat in place.

MAKE THE POCKET FLAPS

1. Align and pin or baste one cut pocket flap and pocket flap lining, with wrong sides together; and apply bias binding to the pocket flap's curved edge. Add a little ease in the binding at the curves to help the binding lie flat when finished. Assemble the second pocket flap the same way.

2. Pin and then baste the pocket flaps to the top edge of the front panel, so they meet at the center topstitching line, leaving a ½" space on each outside edge of the front panel for a seam allowance.

ASSEMBLE AND ATTACH THE SIDE PANEL

1. Align and pin the side pocket and the side pocket lining, with right sides together; and stitch the notched end of the pocket with a ½" seam. Press the seam open; then re-fold the pocket and lining, with wrong sides together. Apply bias binding to the pocket's opposite short edge. The seam allowances at the pocket's top and bottom edges are now clean-finished and won't show when the pocket is attached to the bag.

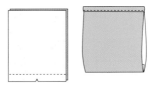

2. Pin the side pocket to one side panel, with right sides up and the pocket's bottom edge aligned with the pocket-placement line and notches on the side panel, as shown. Edgestitch the bottom of the pocket to the side panel; then baste the outside edges of the pocket to the side panel.

3. Repeat steps 1-2 with the second side pocket and side panel.

4. Align and pin the two side panels, with right sides together, and stitch the short edge (the single-notched edge) with a ½" seam. Press the seam allowances to one side; then edgestitch the seam to reinforce it and catch the seam allowances in the stitching. We'll refer to this piece, from here on, as the side panel.

5. Slip the single-loop strap adjuster onto the short strap; then fold the short strap in half to form a loop. Pin or baste the loop's two raw ends together temporarily, as shown at left in the illustration below.

6. Finish one raw end of the long strap with a zigzag stitch. Then feed that end of the strap through the double-strap adjuster (the one that looks like a buckle), so it wraps around the center bar. Stitch a rectangle to secure the strap on itself with a 2" overlap. This will be a bulky seam, so be sure to use a strong needle. Then turn the long strap and double-strap adjuster, so the long strap's zigzagged end faces up, and feed the opposite end of the long strap upwards through the single-strap adjuster, as shown.

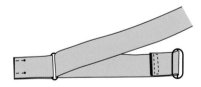

7. Feed the long strap back through both sides of the double-loop strap adjuster. This will create a loop in the long strap, and that strap's zigzagged end will be sandwiched between the loop's layers. The two straps are now connected to make one long strap.

8. Turn the combined strap over to the wrong side, and pin the ends of the doubled short strap to one end of the side panel; and pin the end of the long strap to the opposite end of the side panel. Center the straps between the two placement notches on the ends of the side panel. Baste the ends of the strap to the ends of the side panel with a ¼" seam.

9. Turn the side panel, so the short strap is positioned on the left side and the long strap on the right. Pin one gusset to each end of the side panel, with right sides together, sandwiching the strap between the gusset and side panel. If the bag will be worn by someone who's right-handed, position the gussets' longer edges closest to you. If you're making the bag for someone who's left-handed, position the gussets' shorter edges closest to you (so the hardware will be at the wearer's back). Stitch one end of the side panel, sewing through all the layers with a ½" seam. Press the seam allowances toward the side panel; and edgestitch the seam, catching all the seam allowances in it. Stitch the opposite end of the side panel the same way. The straps, side panel, and gussets now form a large loop, which we'll refer to, from here on, as the side panel.

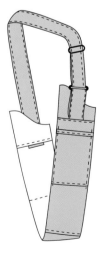

10. Pin the side panel to the front panel, with right sides together, matching the gussets' short edges to the top of the front panel. Pin the side panel's center seam to the center notch at the bottom of the front panel, then continue to pin the side panel to the edge of the front panel, clipping the side panel at the curves to help it fit. Baste the layers; then stitch them in place with a ½" seam.

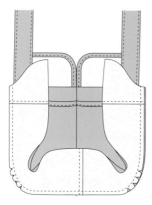

11. Turn the front of the bag right side out.

MAKE AND ATTACH THE INSIDE POCKET

1. Align and pin the two cut inside-pocket pieces, with right sides together. Stitch the perimeter with a ½" seam, starting at the raw edges, rotating at the dots and corners, and leaving an opening for turning the pocket right side out at the bottom between the two dots. (Note that when leaving an opening for turning the pocket right side out, by starting and ending your stitching at the seam allowances' raw edges, the seam allowances will be forced inside the opening when you turn the pocket right side out.) Clip the corners, and trim the seam allowances, except at the opening, to about ¼"; then turn the pocket right side out through the opening. Use a knitting needle or chopstick to gently push out

the corners, and tuck the seam allowances into the opening, so they don't show. Press the pocket flat.

2. Position the inside pocket on the front panel lining at the pocket-placement markings you transferred from the pattern, with the opening at the bottom of the pocket. Edgestitch the sides and bottom of the pocket, which will also close the opening.

3. To divide the pocket into sections, use a ruler and a water-soluble fabric-marking pen or chalk to draw the stitching lines. You can divide the pocket into equal sections, stitching a line down the center; or you can create individual compartments for storing pens and pencils by marking and stitching lines 1" apart, as shown below.

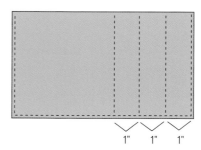

4. Topstitch the lines you've drawn, backstitching or lockstitching at the beginning and end of each seam to secure it.

ASSEMBLE THE LINING

1. Align and pin the two side-panel lining pieces, with right sides together, and stitch the short sides (the single-notched edge) together with a ½" seam. Press the seam allowances open.

2. Attach the side panel lining to the front panel lining the same way you assembled the outside of the bag, with right sides together, matching the shorter sides of the side panel lining to the top edge of the front panel lining and pinning the perimeter. Clip the side panel lining and the curves as needed; then stitch the side panel lining to the front panel lining with a ½" seam.

PREPARE THE BAG FOR ASSEMBLY

1. Tuck the lining inside the front panel, with wrong sides together; and align, pin, and baste the raw edges at the perimeter.

2. Apply bias binding to the top edge of the outside panel and lining, taking care at the curves along the side panel.

ATTACH THE BACK PANEL AND BIAS BINDING

1. Align and pin or baste the back panel lining to the back panel, with wrong sides together.

2. Pin the back panel to the bag, with lining sides together and matching the side panels' notches to the notches at the sides of the back panel. Clip the curves at the side panel to make the side panel fit, if necessary. Baste all the layers together with a ³⁄₈" seam. The raw edges of the back panel and the side panel will show at the outside of the bag, but you'll cover them by applying bias binding to this seam in the next step.

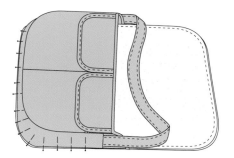

3. Attach bias binding to the perimeter of the back panel, finishing the ends where they meet (see page 128 for more information about finishing the binding's ends).

FINISH THE BAG

1. Remove the basting from the center of the front pocket pleat to let the pleat open up.

2. If you want, add snap closures to the front pockets and flaps.

reversible bucket hat

Hats are a must for covering up young, delicate skin. This one has lots of style and sews up very quickly.

You can make it reversible with two favorite fabrics, or you could add a little pocket on the outside and complement it with a fun lining. Make one. Make two. Make enough to coordinate with each of your child's summer outfits or activities.

When making the hat, you'll sew a curve and apply topstitching. If you're relatively new to sewing but have successfully completed one or two other one-scissors projects in this book, you're definitely ready to take on this one.

SKILLS NEEDED
Sewing curved seam, Edgestitching, Topstitching

FINISHED SIZES
Extra-small, fits 6-12 M, inside crown measurement, 18" (*small,* 12-24 M, 19"; *medium,* 3-5, 20"; *large,* 6-8, 21")

(Measure your child's head to be sure you are making the correct size.)

MATERIALS
FABRIC A: ⅓ yd. of 44"-wide, light- to medium-weight cotton, for one side of hat

FABRIC B: ⅓ yd. of 44"-wide fabric of same type and weight as Fabric A, for other side of hat

½ yd. of medium-weight sew-in interfacing, for brim

Coordinating thread

Hat pattern (see Pattern Sheet 2; Pattern 7, three pieces: A-C)

1. Starting with the cut Fabric A side panels, align and pin the two side panels, with right sides together. Stitch the side seams with a ½" seam; then press the seam allowances open, and trim them to ¼".

2. Pin the crown to the top of the side panels, matching the triple notches on the crown to those on the side panels and the crown's single notches to the side panels' side seams. Clip into the seam allowances of the side panels to make the side panels fit the crown; then join the sides and crown with a ½" seam.

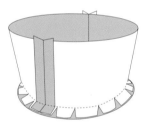

3. Finger-press the seam allowances toward the side panels; then edgestitch the seam allowances to the side panels, if desired, to give the top of the hat a finished look. Trim the remaining seam allowances to ⅛".

4. Repeat steps 1-3 to sew the second cap from Fabric B.

1. Align and pin two cut Fabric A brims, with right sides together; and stitch the sides with a ½" seam. Press the seams open, and trim the seam allowances to ⅛".

2. Align and pin the interfacing pieces to the wrong side of the two Fabric B brims. Then align and pin these two "interfaced" Fabric B brim pieces, with the Fabric B sides together, and join the sides with a ½" seam. Press the seams open, and trim them to ¼", as in Step 1, above.

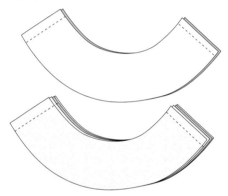

3. Align and pin the interfaced (Fabric B) and un-interfaced (Fabric A) brims, with right sides together. Stitch the outside edges together with a ½" seam; then trim the seam allowances to ⅛".

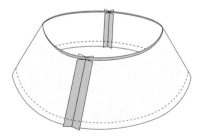

4. Turn the brim right side out, and finger-press the edges before pressing them with an iron. Edgestitch or topstitch the outside edge with a ¼" seam. If you want, you can also topstitch a series of rows around the brim spaced ¼" apart to give the bucket hat a sporty look and add additional stiffness to the brim.

5. Align and pin the brim to the bottom edge of the Fabric A cap, with right sides together and clipping into the brim's seam allowances to make the two edges fit. Stitch through all the layers to attach the brim to the cap with a ½" seam.

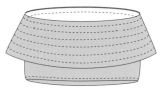

6. Trim the seam allowances to ¼"; then turn the hat wrong side out.

FINISH THE HAT

1. Fold and press the bottom edges of the Fabric B cap toward the wrong side by ½".

2. Fit and pin the Fabric B cap over the Fabric A cap, with wrong sides together and the side seams aligned. Hand-stitch the Fabric B cap's folded edge to the hat with a blindstitch, covering the seam line.

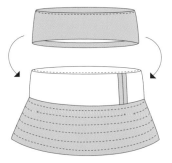

Turn the hat so that the Fabric A side is right side out again, and edgestitch the seam where the side panels and brim meet. This seam will help to secure the two sides of the hat, so they stay together.

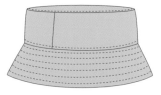

bias-trimmed apron

My sisters and I all had simple, practical aprons like this one when we were growing up. They were sewn by our great aunt in wild 1960s-era cotton prints. I have such fond memories of my childhood apron that I wanted to make a new one for this book—with a few adjustments to improve the fit and wearability. I've slimmed it down a bit, softened the curved shoulder line, and moved the pockets so they are more accessible.

This project calls for a lot of bias binding, so it provides a great opportunity to refine your skills with it. The aprons my great aunt made for us were sewn from quilting cotton, which is lightweight and drapes gently, but for a sturdier apron with better resistance to spills, you might want to try a home-decorating-weight fabric like the one we used for the apron in the photo. Oilcloth would also work well, provided that you use a walking foot or lay tissue paper on the machine bed to prevent the fabric from sticking to your machine as you sew.

SKILLS NEEDED

Applying bias binding

FINISHED SIZES

Small, fits up to size 3 (*medium*, sizes 3-6; *large*, sizes 6-10)

Chest, 24 ½" (30", 33 ½")

Length, 18 ³⁄₈" (22 ⁷⁄₈", 27 ¾")

MATERIALS

NOTE: In cutting dimensions throughout, length precedes width.

¾ yd. (1 ¼ yd., 1 ½ yd.) of 44"-wide, light- to medium-weight fabric like quilting or home-dec-weight cotton, chambray, or linen

4½ yds. (5 yds., 6 yds.) of ³⁄₈"-wide homemade bias binding (see page 126) or 2 packages of ¼"-wide, double-folded, ready-made bias binding

Coordinating thread

2 snaps or ½"-1" Velcro squares or circles

Two 7" x 1" strips of lightweight fusible interfacing

Apron pattern (see Pattern Sheet 2; Pattern 8, four pieces: A-D) and cutting diagram on page 125

1. Follow the manufacturer's instructions to fuse a 7" x 1" strip of lightweight interfacing to the wrong side of each apron back where you transferred the pattern markings.

2. Fold and press each apron back's center-back edge twice to the wrong side, first by ½", and then by 1". Edgestitch the innermost fold to finish the plackets.

PREPARE THE SIDE PANELS

1. Apply bias binding to the top edge (the narrowest edge) of both pocket pieces (see "Working with bias binding" on page 126).

2. Apply bias binding to the top edge (the narrowest edge) of both side panels.

3. With the right sides together, align the pocket's bottom edge with the notches at the sides of the side panel. Stitch the pocket's bottom edge to the side panel with a ¼" seam.

4. Press the pocket toward the top of the side panel (covering the pocket's seam allowance and stitching), and edgestitch the seam on the pocket's right side.

5. Baste the sides of the pocket to the edges of the side panel with a ¼" seam.

6. Staystitch the neckline of the front and back apron panels ¼" from the raw edge. Note that the staystitching will not be shown in the illustrations.

ASSEMBLE THE APRON

1. Join the shoulders with a French seam to give the inside of the smock a clean, finished appearance. To make the French seam, align and pin the front and back panels with wrong sides together. Stitch the shoulders with a ¼" seam; then trim the seam allowances to ⅛", press the seam allowances open, and re-pin the shoulders with right sides facing, sandwiching the seam allowances between the layers. Stitch the shoulders again with a ¼" seam to encase the seam allowances' raw edges. Press the finished seam allowances toward the apron back.

2. Align and pin both side panels to the front panel, with wrong sides facing, matching the raw edges at the bottom of the pieces and also the top of the side panels to the notches on the front panel. Baste the front and sides together with a ¼" seam.

3. Align and pin the opposite edge of each side panel to the corresponding back panel, with wrong sides together and matching the top of the side panels to the back panel's notches. Baste the backs and sides together with a ¼" seam.

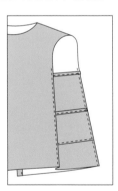

APPLY THE BIAS BINDING

1. Starting at a lower edge of one side panel, apply bias binding up one side of the side panel, around the curved edge of the armhole, and down the other side of the side panel. Trim the ends of the binding flush with the apron's hem. The ends can remain unfinished since they'll be enclosed in the bias binding that you'll add at the hem in Step 4 below.

2. Repeat Step 1 to apply bias binding to the other side panel and shoulder.

3. At the apron's hem edge, press the side panel bias bindings toward the side panels, and pin them in place temporarily.

4. Apply bias binding to the hem of the apron, starting at one center-back edge and ending at the opposite center-back edge. Remember to fold under the ends of the binding before applying it to the hem to clean-finish the apron's center-back edges.

5. Apply bias binding to the apron's neck edge, folding under and finishing the ends of the binding at the center-back of the apron.

FINISH THE APRON

1. Apply snaps or Velcro at the placement markings that you transferred from the pattern.

bento box carrier

Bento boxes are Japanese-style lunch boxes with individual compartments for different types of food—a presentation that can entice even the pickiest preschooler to finish lunch. They can be purchased in different sizes at Japanese grocery stores and online. We designed this carrier to hold most child-sized bento boxes.

This carrier does double duty; it makes transporting the bento box easy and also opens up into a cute vinyl-covered placemat that you can embellish in all sorts of creative ways. Instead of the fork and spoon that we've added to the inside of the carrier (see the photo on page 43), why not appliqué some chopsticks and sushi to give it real Japanese flair?

SKILLS NEEDED
Applying bias binding, Working with fusible appliqué

FINISHED SIZE
About 8 ½" x 6" x 4", excluding handle; fits average-sized (7" x 5" x 2") bento box

MATERIALS
NOTE: In cutting dimensions throughout, length precedes width.

FABRIC A: ¼ yd. of 44"-wide, lightweight fabric like quilting cotton, for exterior

FABRIC B: 10" square of quilting cotton, for handle lining

FABRIC C: ¼ yd. of 44"-wide, quilting cotton, for vinyl-covered placemat and inside gussets

¼ yd. of 44"-wide clear vinyl, for inside of bag

Fabric scraps, for appliqué (optional)

3 yds. of ⅜"-wide homemade bias binding (see page 126) or 1 package of ½"-wide, double-folded, ready-made bias binding

10" square of lightweight, non-woven fusible interfacing

10" square of fusible appliqué web (see Resources on page 134) (optional)

Coordinating thread

5" length of ¾"-wide Velcro

Tissue paper

1 sheet of rigid vinyl template plastic (see Resources on page 134)

Glue stick

Sandpaper

Bento Box pattern (see Pattern Sheet 1; Pattern 3, six pieces: A–F)

1. Cut out two inside-handle pattern pieces from lightweight fusible interfacing, and carefully trace and trim the inside of the handle shape from the interfacing. The edge of the interfacing will serve as a stitching guide, so trim it smoothly and close to the traced line. Then align and fuse each of the interfacing pieces to the wrong side of the two cut-fabric inside handles.

2. Align and pin one interfaced inside handle to one end of the outside panel, with right sides together and matching the raw edges. Carefully stitch the center edge of the handle, using the interfacing as a guide. Take your time at the curves.

3. Carefully cut through both the handle and outside panel in the center of the handle, and trim all the layers of fabric to about ⅛" from your stitching. Clip into the seam allowances close to the stitching line at the curves, taking care not to cut into the stitching itself.

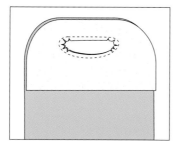

4. Turn the handle right side out, pulling the inside handle fabric through the hole you've cut. Gently finger-press the hole's seam before pressing it with an iron, making sure both layers of fabric are smooth.

5. To prepare the plastic inside handle, carefully trim the center of the handle, using sandpaper on its inside edge to smooth its curves. Position the plastic inside handle on top of the inside handle, with the handle openings aligned. Then pull just the fabric handle through the opening on the plastic inside handle, and adjust the layers so that both fabric layers are smooth. The template plastic is now sandwiched between the inside handle and the outside panel fabric. You can use a glue stick to temporarily adhere the fabric layers to the template plastic before edgestitching the handle to secure all the layers.

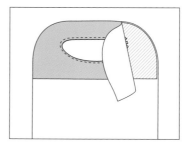

6. Cut a 3" length of Velcro, and position it on the Velcro-placement markings you transferred from the pattern to the cut inside handle. To stitch the Velcro in place, fold the outside fabric out of the way so you only stitch the Velcro to the interfaced inside handle and the template plastic.

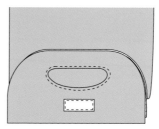

7. Repeat steps 2-6 to make the opposite handle of the carrier.

Because the inside of the carrier is lined with clear vinyl to protect it from spills, the appliqué process is very simple: You can simply fuse decorations to the fabric without adding the usual stitching around the appliqué's raw edges, so have fun with this step. You'll cut the plate, fork, and spoon from a fusible web, which acts like a thin layer of glue when heated; and after deciding where you want to position the pieces, you'll iron them in place (fusible-interfacing side down) to attach them to the lining. You can add stitching details, like the prongs of the fork, or add other embellishments, like green peas on one side of the plate—some of which you may want to position as having even spilled off the plate! The recipient might enjoy being involved in designing these embellishments.

1. Trace the shape of the fork, spoon, and plate onto the paper liner of the paper-backed appliqué web. Then follow the manufacturer's directions to fuse the web to the wrong side of the appliqué fabric.

2. Cut the fabric and the fusible web along the traced lines. Then peel the paper liner from the web, leaving the web on the fabric itself.

3. Position the appliqués on the right side of the lining fabric; and once you're happy with the placement, follow the manufacturer's directions to fuse them to the lining.

4. If you want, add details to the appliqué with embroidery stitches, machine stitching, or additional appliqué.

ASSEMBLE THE CARRIER

1. Position the vinyl lining over the right side of the embellished (or plain, if you prefer) lining fabric. Place a layer of tissue paper on the sewing-machine bed to keep the vinyl from sticking to the machine as you sew, and lay the carrier vinyl side down under the needle to baste it to the lining fabric (positioning it vinyl side down enables you to see the fabric's edge as you sew). Baste the perimeter of the vinyl and lining fabric together with a ¼" seam, take the work out of the machine, and tear the tissue paper away from the stitching.

2. Flip both handles toward the outside of the carrier, and align and pin just the inside handle fabric to the vinyl-covered lining, with right sides together. Stitch the edges with a ½" seam. The outside of the carrier will be longer than the lining and can be folded out of the way, as shown.

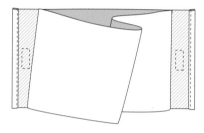

3. Finger-press the seam allowances toward the handle side, and turn the carrier right side out. Check to be sure all the layers of the handle (including the seam allowances) are lying flat. Then topstitch through all the layers, ¼" from the lining seam to secure the handles.

4. Baste the perimeter of the carrier with a ¼" seam; then trim any uneven edges from the perimeter in preparation for applying the bias binding.

MAKE THE GUSSETS

1. Align all three layers of one gusset, so the wrong sides of the outside fabric and lining fabric face together and the clear vinyl covers the lining fabric. Pin the layers together in the seam allowances to keep the pins from marring the vinyl that will be visible in the gusset itself. Cover the sewing-machine bed with tissue paper to prevent the vinyl from sticking to the machine, lay the gusset vinyl side down under the needle, and baste the perimeter with a ¼" seam.

2. Position the gusset vinyl side up in the machine, and begin applying the ⅜" bias binding (see "Working with bias binding" on page 126 for more information on making and applying bias binding) to the vinyl side of the gusset's curved edge. As you sew the curves, remember to ease in a little extra binding at the outside curves and stretch the binding a bit at the inside curves. This will help the binding fit better when finished. Then place another piece of tissue paper on the machine bed; turn the gusset vinyl side down, so the outside fabric faces up; and fold and stitch the binding to the outside of the gusset to finish it.

3. Trim the ends of the binding flush with the gusset's straight edges. Then repeat steps 1-3 with the second gusset.

4. Using the placement markings you transferred from the pattern piece, stitch a 2" piece of Velcro to the outside of one gusset and to the lining side of the other gusset.

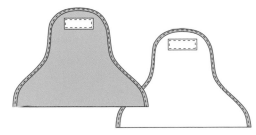

FINISH THE CARRIER

1. Pin the gussets to the carrier (pinning in the seam allowances only), with vinyl sides together. Align the raw edges and notches at the center of the pieces, and baste each of the gussets to the carrier with a ¼" seam.

2. Apply the ⅜" bias binding to the entire perimeter of the carrier, starting on the vinyl/lining side and finishing the binding on the outside. Remember to lay tissue paper on the machine bed when you turn the carrier over to sew on the outside of the carrier to prevent the vinyl from sticking to the machine.

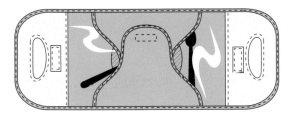

play town

It's amazing how easy it is to assemble a simple street scene or even a whole town using these basic building block shapes and a little bit of ingenuity.

Be creative and watch what happens. Stack two brownstones on top of each other and you've got a high-rise. Want a more suburban feel? Turn a brownstone on its side and you've made a ranch-style house. Throw in some toy cars and other props and you've found a way to occupy a couple of rambunctious kids on a rainy afternoon.

Use these ideas or look around at buildings and houses in your neighborhood to find your own sources of inspiration. Caution: It's easy to get completely carried away with this project!

SKILLS NEEDED
Appliqué, Hand-stitching

FINISHED SIZES
HOUSE:
3¾" x 3¾" x 5⅜"

BROWNSTONE:
3¾" x 3¾" x 6¼"

MATERIALS
NOTE: In dimensions throughout, unless otherwise noted, length precedes width.

FABRIC A: ¼ yd. of light- to mid-weight cotton fabric, like quilting or home-dec-weight cotton, or lightweight canvas, for walls and base of house

FABRIC B: 7" x 5" of similar fabric, for house roof

FABRIC C: ¼ yd. or 1 fat quarter (18" wide x 21" long) of similar fabric for wall, base, and roof of brownstone

Quilting-cotton scraps, for windows, doors, and other decorations

Fusible appliqué web (see Resources on page 134)

Coordinating thread

9" x 7" rectangle of 4"-thick foam (makes 2 buildings)

Knitting needle or chopstick

Serrated or electric knife, for cutting foam

Water-soluble fabric-marking pen

Play Town pattern (see Pattern Sheet 1; Pattern 4, eight pieces: A-H)

When assembling the house and brownstone, begin and end your stitching at the dots you transferred from the pattern, ½" from the raw edges. This will make it easier to fit the pieces together when the brownstone's roof and base or the house's faces are added. Also remember to backstitch or lockstitch at the beginning and end of each seam to secure the stitches.

PREPARE THE HOUSE

1. Align and pin the two cut roof pieces, with right sides together, and join them along one long edge with a ½" seam, starting and stopping at the dots you transferred from the pattern piece. Press the seam allowances open.

2. Align and pin the two house walls to the roof's unstitched long edges, with right sides together, and join them with a ½" seam. Press the seam allowances open. The four assembled pieces should form a long rectangle with the roof at center. Baste a row of stitches along the lower edge of each house wall and each of the two house faces ½" from the raw edge. The basting will serve as a stitching guide when it's time to hand-stitch the house closed after inserting the foam.

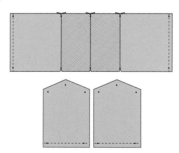

PREPARE THE BROWNSTONE

1. Align and pin two brownstone walls, with right sides together, and join them along one long edge with a ½" seam, starting and stopping at the dots

you transferred from the pattern piece. Repeat this step to join the other two walls.

2. With right sides together, join the two sets of walls along one edge with a ½" seam, so all four walls are connected in a long row. Press the seam allowances open. Baste along the lower edge of the brownstone's walls ½" from the raw edge. This basting will serve as a stitching guide when it's time to hand-stitch the brownstone closed after inserting the foam.

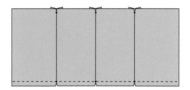

MAKE THE WINDOWS

1. Using the window appliqué pattern as a template, draw or trace the window's shape on the fusible web's paper liner for as many windows as you want on your house or brownstone. Then follow the manufacturer's directions to fuse the web to the wrong side of the window-appliqué fabrics.

2. Cut the fabric and fusible web along the traced lines. Then peel the liner from the web, leaving the web on the fabric itself.

3. Position the windows on the right side of the house or brownstone fabric, using the markings you transferred from the patterns. Once you're happy with the placement, follow the manufacturer's directions to fuse the windows to the fabric.

4. Satin-stitch the raw edges of each window. Pivot at each corner, or cut your thread and stitch a separate row of zigzag stitches for each side of the window. Repeat this step for the remaining windows.

5. If you want, add additional details to each window by machine-stitching window mullions with a straight stitch. You might also want to add other ornamentation with embroidery stitches, machine stitching, or additional appliqué.

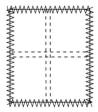

MAKE THE DOOR

1. Align and pin the two door pieces, with right sides together. Stitch the perimeter with a ¼" seam, starting at the raw edges and pivoting at the first transferred dot, then pivoting at each corner, and finally pivoting and stitching back to the raw edges after reaching the second dot. You'll use the opening between the two dots for turning the door right side out later.

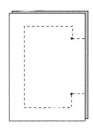

2. Clip the corners, and trim the seam allowances to about ⅛", leaving the opening's edges untrimmed; then turn the door right side out through the opening. Use a knitting needle or chopstick to gently push out the corners, and tuck the seam allowances into the opening so they don't show. Press the door flat.

3. Machine-stitch the door's outline on the house or brownstone fabric using the door-placement marking you transferred from the pattern to make a frame for the door when opened. If you prefer, instead of stitching a door frame, you can appliqué a fabric scrap cut in the shape of the door (with the seam allowances trimmed away) to form an open doorway. To do this, follow the fusing instructions above for the windows.

4. Pin the fabric door into position on the right side of the house or brownstone fabric over the top-stitched or appliquéd doorway, and edgestitch the door's left edge to the building, simultaneously closing up the opening left for turning the door right side out as you attach the door.

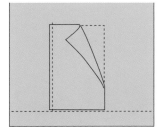

5. After embellishing the brownstone, finish assembling it using the directions in "Begin to assemble the brownstone" on page 51.

BEGIN TO ASSEMBLE THE HOUSE

1. Align and pin the walls and roof of the house to one house face, with right sides together, matching the dots and raw edges. Then stitch one side edge at a time, sewing precisely to the dots.

2. Repeat Step 1 to attach the second house face.

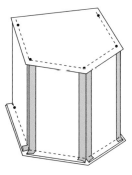

3. Finger-press the seam allowances open. The house is now completely assembled except for the base.

1. Align and pin the two unstitched walls of the brownstone, with right sides together, and join them with a ½" seam, starting and stopping your stitching at the dots. Press the seam allowances open.

2. Align and pin the brownstone's roof to the walls, with right sides together, matching the raw edges at the dots. Then stitch one edge at a time, stitching precisely to the dots.

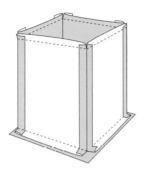

3. Finger-press the seam allowances open. The brownstone is now completely assembled except for the base.

1. Fold and press three raw edges of the base for the house or brownstone to the wrong side by ½".

2. Align and pin the base's fourth unfolded edge to one of the building's bottom edges, matching the raw edges and dots, and join the two with a ½" seam.

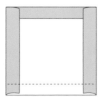

3. Trace the foam template from the pattern sheet onto the foam with a ball-point or felt-tipped pen. Then use a serrated knife to cut the foam, using long, smooth strokes for a clean cut. The foam shape is slightly larger than the finished building, so don't worry if the foam isn't perfect; it will be compressed to the shape of the building.

4. With the house or brownstone wrong side out, place its roof on top of the foam shape, and gradually turn the building right side out as you gently pull it over the foam shape. Because the foam is cut slightly larger than the building itself, it will be a snug fit.

5. Shape the building, tugging on the edges and corners to square them against the foam. Use a knitting needle or chopstick to help push out the corners.

6. Using the basting stitches you sewed earlier along the walls' bottom edges as a guide for pinning and stitching, pin the folded edges of the base over the raw edges of the walls and hand-stitch the opening closed with a blindstitch.

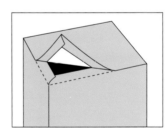

penguin backpack

My husband took our daughter to Paris when she was young. Shortly before they left, I came across a fabric printed with a map of Paris and used it to make her a backpack for the trip. We filled it with toys for the flight and, upon arrival, she and her dad pretended to use the map to navigate around the city.

The Paris Backpack, as we came to call it, served as the inspiration for this project when I realized that it could be made into a cute penguin with some simple embellishments. Follow the instructions here to create a penguin, use your imagination to create another creature (perhaps a ladybug), or find a fabric that does the thematic work for you (like the Paris fabric did for me) and leave off the embellishments entirely.

SKILLS NEEDED
Sewing curved seam, Topstitching, Installing zipper

FINISHED SIZE
12" x 9½" x 3½"

MATERIALS
NOTE: In dimensions throughout, unless otherwise noted, length precedes width.

FABRIC A: 1 yd. of 44"-wide, medium-weight fabric that's somewhat stiff but not too bulky, like home-dec-weight fabric, denim, canvas, or cotton twill, for backpack and straps

FABRIC B: ¾ yd. of 44"-wide quilting cotton, for lining and inside pocket

FABRIC C: ¼ yd. of 44"-wide or a fat quarter (18" wide x 21" long) of quilting or home-dec-weight cotton, for penguin feet and beak (optional)

FABRIC D: 14" x 7" of quilting or home-dec-weight cotton, for front belly pocket (optional)

½ yd. of lightweight fusible interfacing

One 18" closed-end, molded-tooth (Vislon) zipper or nylon zipper (not an invisible zipper)

Two 1" buttons, for eyes (optional)

Two 1½"-wide strap adjusters (see Resources on page 134)

Coordinating thread

Water-soluble fabric-marking pen or chalk

Knitting needle or chopstick

Zipper foot or walking foot

Backpack pattern (see Pattern Sheet 4; Pattern 16, fifteen pieces: A-O) and cutting diagram on page 124; plus two 21" x 6" pieces from Fabric A (no pattern piece provided for long straps)

1. Trace the stitching lines from the penguin foot pattern on the wrong side of one cut fabric foot.

2. Align and pin the traced foot to another cut foot, with right sides together. Stitch the two feet together along the traced stitching line, pivoting at the corners and dots and backstitching at the beginning and end of the seam. Note that if you take one stitch across the tip of each of the two center toes, from one dot to the next, you'll have created nice points when you turn the foot right side out. Leave the top edge of the foot open for turning it right side out.

3. Trim the seam allowances, except at the opening, to ⅛", and clip the corners. Then turn the foot right side out, using a chopstick or knitting needle to gently push out the corners. Finger-press the edges; then press the foot with an iron, and lay it aside.

4. Repeat steps 1-3 to make the second foot, and likewise trace, stitch, turn, and press the beak and two wings.

1. Align and pin the two front belly pocket pieces, with right sides together, and stitch their perimeter

with a ½" seam, starting and ending your stitching at the fabric's raw edges and pivoting at the stitching line and at the dots you transferred from the pattern. Leave an opening between the two notches at the top edge for turning the pocket right side out.

When leaving an opening for turning the pocket right side out, it's a good idea to start and end your stitching at the raw edge of the seam allowance, as shown in the illustration below, pivoting when you reach the seam line. By sewing across the seam allowances, they'll be forced inside the opening when you turn the pocket right side out.

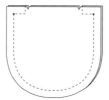

2. Trim the pocket's seam allowances (except for those at the opening) to ⅛", and clip the corners. Then turn the pocket right side out through the opening. Finger-press the edges; then press them with an iron.

3. Hand-stitch the opening closed with a blindstitch. Then position the pocket on the front panel at the markings you transferred from the pattern, and pin it in place. Edgestitch or satin-stitch the pocket's curved edge to the front panel to finish it (satin stitching will give the pocket edge a neat appearance).

4. Align and pin the beak to the top edge of the front panel, matching the center notches; and baste the beak in place with a ³⁄₈" seam. Pin the top open edge of each foot to the bottom edge of the front panel, matching the notches; and baste them in place with a ³⁄₈" seam.

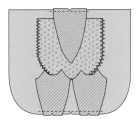

5. Pin the top front panel to the front panel, with right sides together, so the beak is sandwiched between the two pieces; and stitch them with a ½" seam. Use your zipper foot to stitch this seam if the front belly pocket interferes with your stitching. Press the seam allowances toward the top front panel; then set the backpack front aside temporarily.

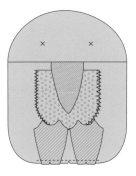

INSERT THE ZIPPER

1. Cut two strips of fusible interfacing 17" x 1 ½". Fuse one interfacing strip to the wrong side of one cut zipper panel along one long raw edge. Repeat with the second cut zipper panel and interfacing strip. Align and pin the two interfaced edges of the zipper panels together; then baste them with a ½" seam.

2. Press the seam allowances open. On the right side of the fabric, use a water-soluble fabric-marking pen or chalk to mark the zipper stitching line ³⁄₈" on each side of the basted center line. Working from the wrong side of the basted zipper panels, start pinning the zipper so that it's centered on the seam line. Work with the top side of the zipper facing the wrong side of the zipper panels, and center the zipper on the basted seam. The top of the zipper teeth should start ½" from the raw edges of the zipper panels' short ends. Hand-baste the zipper to the basted zipper panels.

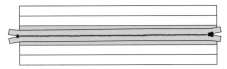

3. Remove the basting from the panel's center seam (the basting from Step 1 above), so the zipper is exposed from the right side and the two panels are separated. Then, using your zipper foot (or a walking foot with the needle moved to one side, so you can stitch about ³⁄₈" from the folded edge of the zipper panel) and starting from the top of the zipper, topstitch both sides of the zipper from the right side along the stitching lines you marked in Step 2 above.

ASSEMBLE THE SIDE PANEL

1. Pin one wing to one end of the side panel, matching the notches, and baste the layers together with a ³⁄₈" seam. Baste the second wing to the opposite end of the side panel.

2. Pin the zipper panel to the side panel, with right sides together, sandwiching the wings between the two layers. With the zipper panel facing up (so you can see the back of the zipper), sew the ends of the layers together with a ½" seam. When your stitching reaches

the edge of the zipper teeth, lift the needle, raising the presser foot just a little; and skip over the teeth before you resume stitching (stitching over the zipper teeth will break your needle). The backpack's side panel is now sewn together in one long loop.

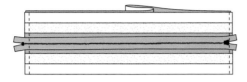

MAKE THE STRAPS

1. From Fabric A, cut two 21" x 6" strips for the long straps. Fold one of the 21" x 6" strips in half lengthwise, with wrong sides together, and press the crease to create a center fold line.

2. Open the strap, and lay it flat and wrong side up. Fold each long raw edge in toward the center crease, and press the folds.

3. Fold the strap in half again (along the center crease line formed in Step 1), and press it, enclosing its raw edges in the fold. The strap is now folded into four fabric thicknesses.

4. Edgestitch the strap near the long open edge, and edgestitch it again along the opposite folded edge to finish it.

5. Repeat steps 1-4 to prepare the other long strap, the two short straps, and the hanger strap.

ASSEMBLE THE BACK PANEL

1. Slip the center bar of a strap adjuster onto one short strap, and then fold the strap in half to form a loop. Pin or baste the loop's two raw ends to the bottom edge of the back panel between the outer set of notches. Repeat with the second short strap.

2. Pin or baste one raw end of one long strap to the top edge of the back panel between the outer pair of notches. Repeat with the second long strap.

3. Align and pin the top back panel to the top edge of the back panel, with right sides together (the long straps will be sandwiched between the two layers); and join the pair with a ½" seam.

4. Press the seam allowances toward the top of the backpack; then edgestitch the seam to help secure the straps.

5. Baste the ends of the hanger strap to the top edge of the backpack between each pair of notches.

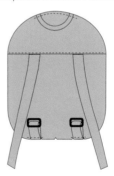

ASSEMBLE THE BACKPACK

1. Pin the side panel to the back panel, starting at the center bottom and center top of the bag and matching the notches as you go. If necessary, clip the side panel at the curves to help the two pieces fit together; then join the pair with a ½" seam.

2. Repeat Step 1 with the front panel, making sure to open the zipper beforehand, so you'll have a way to turn the backpack right side out when you've finished stitching.

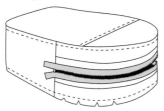

3. Turn the backpack right side out, and stitch the button eyes to the front panel at the markings you transferred from the pattern.

1. Fuse interfacing to the wrong side of one cut inside pocket piece, following the manufacturer's fusing instructions.

2. Align and pin the two inside pocket pieces, with right sides together. Stitch the perimeter, pivoting at the corners and leaving an opening at the bottom between the two notches for turning the pocket right side out. Clip the corners, and trim the seam allowances, except along the opening, to approximately ⅛". Then turn the pocket right side out through the opening, using a knitting needle or chopstick to gently push out the corners; and tuck the seam allowances into the opening so they don't show. Finger-press the edges before pressing them with an iron.

3. Position the inside pocket on one lining panel at the pocket-placement markings you transferred from the pattern, with the opening for turning the pocket right side out placed at the bottom of the pocket. Edgestitch the sides and bottom of the pocket to secure it, closing up the opening.

4. Use a water-soluble fabric-marking pen or chalk to draw a center stitching line to divide the pocket in half; or, if you want, draw additional stitching lines 1" apart on half of the pocket for pens and pencils.

5. Topstitch the lines you've drawn, backstitching or lockstitching at the beginning and end of each seam to secure it.

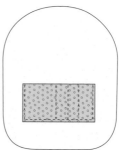

1. Fold and press one long edge of one cut zipper-panel lining to the wrong side by ½". Repeat the process with the other cut zipper-panel lining.

2. Pin the short sides of the two zipper-panel lining pieces to the short side of the side panel, with right sides together (there will be a gap of about ⅝" between the zipper panel lining pieces where the edges have been folded under). Stitch the ends with a ½" seam.

3. Stitch the opposite end of the top zipper panel to the lining side panel the same way. You should now have a lining side-panel loop similar to the one you created for the outside of the backpack earlier.

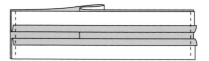

4. Pin and stitch the lining side panel to the lining front and back the same way you assembled the backpack, matching the notches and clipping into the side lining as needed in order to match the curves.

1. Turn both the backpack and the backpack lining wrong side out. Lay them next to each other so that the bottoms of the two shapes touch and the inside pocket and the penguin front both face down. Join the seam allowances of the lining and the bag together at the base for 3"-4" with a ¼" seam. Turn the two bags over, and stitch the opposite side of the base the same way.

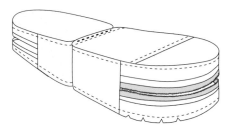

2. Turn the backpack right side out, and tuck the lining inside the bag. Then pull the top of the lining out of the way, so the seam allowances at the top of the bag and the bag lining are exposed. Again, stitch the seam allowances of the lining to the seam allowances of the bag for about 10". Stitch the seam allowances on the opposite side of the bag the same way. By stitching the lining to the backpack at the seam allowances, the lining will be secured to the backpack and will stay in place when the bag is used.

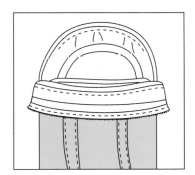

3. Turn the bag opening wrong side out so that the wrong side of the zipper is exposed. Pin the folded edges of the lining zipper panel to the inside of the bag at the zippered edge. Hand-stitch the lining to the zipper tape with a blindstitch to finish it.

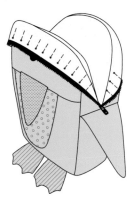

1. Feed the long straps through the strap adjusters. Then check the length of the straps, and trim them as necessary. For a clean finish, remove 1"-2" of edgestitching at each strap's end, and fold the strap's raw ends inside the strap before re-folding and re-stitching the edges and end of the strap. Alternatively you can simply zigzag the straps' ends for an easy, less bulky finish.

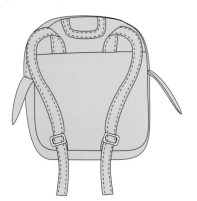

art smock

I designed this smock with the young artist in mind. The elasticized neck and sleeves make it both protective and comfortable to wear, and Velcro or snap closures make it quick and easy to put on and take off. The raglan sleeves are easier to sew than set-in sleeves and make the smock roomy enough to fit over bulky items like sweaters and sweatshirts. The long sleeve length is plain-old practical because, let's face it, most budding artists will inevitably drag their arms through wet paint.

SKILLS NEEDED

Sewing curved seam, Sewing French seam, Edgestitching

FINISHED SIZES

Small, fits up to size 3 (*medium*, sizes 4-6; *large*, sizes 7-10)

Length from shoulder at neckline, 20" (24 ¼", 29")

Sleeve length from center back, 20" (24 ½", 28 ¼")

MATERIALS

NOTE: In cutting dimensions throughout, length precedes width.

FABRIC A: 1 yd. (1 ¼ yds., 1 ¾ yds.) of 44"-wide, lightweight fabric, like quilting cotton, chambray, or linen, for front and back

FABRIC B: 1 yd. (1 ¼ yds., 1 ¼ yds.) of 44"-wide, lightweight fabric like quilting cotton, chambray, or linen, for sleeves, pockets, and neck trim

Two 7" x 1" strips of lightweight fusible interfacing

1 yd. of ⅜"-wide elastic

2 snaps or ½"-1" Velcro patches

Coordinating thread

Bodkin or safety pin

Art Smock pattern (see Pattern Sheet 3; Pattern 11, five pieces: A-E) and cutting diagram on page 125

1. To hem the pocket, fold and press the top edge of one cut pocket to the wrong side by ½". Then fold the top edge again, this time to the right side by 1", and pin it. Stitch the side edges of the pocket at the folds with a ½" seam, as shown in the illustration.

2. Turn the pocket's resulting hem to the wrong side, and press it. Fold the pocket's side and bottom edges toward the wrong side by ½" as well, and press them.

3. Open up the folded seam allowances at the lower corners of the pocket, and fold the corners at a 45-degree angle. Then re-fold the sides. The angled corners will help to give the right side of the pocket a finished appearance.

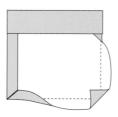

4. Edgestitch the pocket's hem at the inside folded edge. Then pin the pocket to the front smock at the placement dots that you transferred from the pattern; and edgestitch it in place, backstitching or lockstitching at the beginning and end of the seam to secure your stitching and also pivoting at the corners.

> **HINT:** To reinforce and strengthen each pocket, stitch a small triangle in its top corners as you're topstitching the pocket in place.

NOTE: We suggest making this smock with French seams because they give the inside of the smock a clean, finished appearance. A French seam is made by stitching the seam twice—first, stitching it with wrong sides together; then trimming the seam allowances, folding the fabric over the seam allowances so the fabric's wrong sides are together, and finally stitching the seam a second time. This second stitching of the seam encases the seam allowances inside the seam. You'll find full instructions below.

1. Pin one raglan sleeve to the smock front, with wrong sides together and matching the edges and the notch (note that the sleeve has one notch on its front edge and two notches on its back edge, so be sure to join the correct sleeve edge to each side of the smock front). Stitch the sleeve to the smock with a ¼" seam, backstitching at the beginning and end of the seam to secure the stitches.

2. Trim the seam allowances to ⅛", and press them open. Fold the sleeve and front together again over the new seam, so their right sides are facing; and pin the edge in place. Then stitch the seam again, this time ¼" from the pinned edge. This second seam neatly encases the seam allowances' raw edges.

3. Follow steps 1-2 to attach the second sleeve to the smock front's opposite side. Then attach the two back-smock pieces to the opposite edges of the raglan sleeves, again with wrong sides together and following steps 1-2 above.

4. Press the French seam's encased seam allowances toward the center front on the front raglan seam and toward the sleeve on the back raglan seam. This will help to reduce the side seams' bulk when they're sewn in the next step.

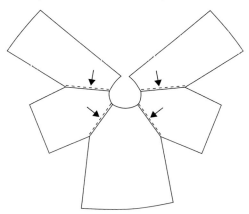

SEW THE SIDE SEAMS WITH FRENCH SEAMS

1. Align and pin the front and backs of the smock, with wrong sides together and the sides and sleeve edges matching. Stitch each side and sleeve seam with a continuous ¼" seam; then trim the seam allowance to ⅛", and press the seam allowances

open. Re-fold the fabric so that the right sides are together, and again stitch a ¼" seam to form a French seam.

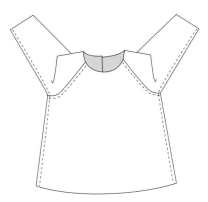

FINISH THE SLEEVES

1. Turn the sleeves wrong side out to make folding and pressing the hem edge easier. Then fold and press each sleeve's raw edge twice to the wrong side—first, by ¼" and then by a generous ½"—to form the casing for the elastic. Edgestitch, leaving a 1"-2" opening near the sleeve seam for feeding the elastic through the casing.

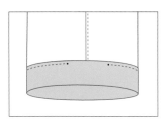

2. Pin a bodkin or safety pin to one end of a 6" (7 ½", 8") length of ⅜"-wide elastic, and feed the elastic into the casing through the opening. Work the elastic's pinned end through the casing and back out the opening, making sure to keep the elastic untwisted in the casing and to keep from pulling its opposite end into the casing as you work. Then pin the two ends of the elastic together, so they overlap by about ½". Stitch the elastic's overlapped, pinned ends together with a tiny rectangle or a bartack to secure them.

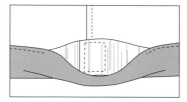

3. Finish edgestitching the casing to close the opening.

HEM THE SMOCK

1. Trim the French seam at each side seam for 2" at the smock's hem, so this section of the side seam is about half the width of the French seam. This will help to reduce bulk when you fold and hem the smock.

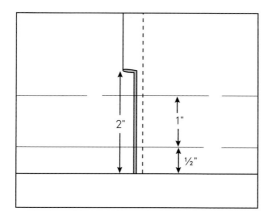

2. Fold and press the hem twice to the wrong side— first, by ½" and then by 1" to encase the bottom edge. Pin the hem, easing the extra fullness from the flare of the hem as you pin. Use your iron to steam the fullness into the hem; then edgestitch the hem's innermost fold to finish it.

ASSEMBLE THE NECKLINE AND FINISH THE SMOCK

1. Follow the manufacturer's instructions to fuse a 7" x 1" strip of interfacing to the wrong side of each smock back's placket edge, following the placement markings you transferred from the pattern.

2. Fold and press one of the smock back's center-back edges toward the wrong side by ½", and press it.

3. Fold and press the same smock back edge a second time, this time toward the right side by 1"; and pin the folds to hold them in place temporarily.

4. Repeat steps 1-3 to prepare the same edge on the other smock back.

5. Fold and press one long edge of the bias strip to the wrong side by ¼". Then fold and press one short end of the bias strip to the wrong side by ½".

6. Align and pin the bias strip's unfolded, long raw edge to the smock's neckline, with right sides together, by pinning the folded short end so that it meets the placket fold, as shown in the illustration on facing page. Take care not to stretch the bias as you pin, and stop pinning about 2" from the smock's opposite folded back placket edge. Fold the bias strip's unfolded short end, so its crease meets the folded edge of the back placket, as you did with the beginning folded end of the bias strip; and trim the excess at the newly folded end of the bias strip so that its seam allowance is ½".

7. Stitch the entire length of the neckline with a ¼" seam, backstitching or lockstitching at the beginning and end of the seam.

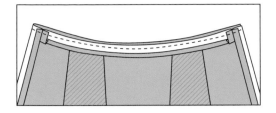

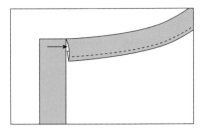

8. Turn the bias strip and back plackets to the smock's wrong side, pushing out the corners at the back neckline. Then re-fold and press the back smock's center-back edge to form the placket. When folded and pressed to the smock's wrong side, the bias strip will not show on the smock's right side.

9. Stitch the long folded edge of the bias strip to the smock to make the casing for the neckline elastic, backstitching at the beginning and end of the seam. Lift the placket out of the way, so it doesn't get stitched in this step, and leave the ends of the casing open so that you can insert the elastic.

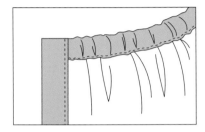

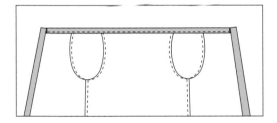

10. Pin a bodkin or safety pin to one end of a 13" (14", 15") length of elastic, and feed the elastic through the casing, also pinning the elastic's ends to the smock so that they don't get pulled through the casing. Adjust the elastic to the desired length; then tuck the ends of the elastic underneath the fold of the placket, and pin and edgestitch the placket's folded edge to finish it neatly and simultaneously catch and anchor the ends of the elastic. This will give the placket a neat, finished look.

11. Apply a snap or a ½"- 1" piece of Velcro at each of the placement markings you transferred from the pattern, so the smock will be easy to put on and take off. Sew the soft part of the Velcro to the wrong side of the smock placket and the scratchy part to the right side on the opposite placket.

cozy winter hood

Sometimes during winter months we have a hard time distinguishing my daughter from her favorite toy. When it's cold outside, she likes to wear a knitted white hat with ears on it that makes her look suspiciously like her stuffed friend Bear.

This hood, inspired by her hat, is shown in a wool coating with a velveteen lining. But it could also be made in microfiber fleece or even lightweight wool felt repurposed from an old sweater. By altering the shape of the ear pieces slightly, our bear could be transformed into other furry friends: long skinny ears make a rabbit; squat triangular ears make a cat; larger oblong floppy ears turn it into a dog.

SKILLS NEEDED

Sewing curved seam,
Hand-stitching

FINISHED SIZES

Extra small, fits most infants up to 12 M (*small*, 12 M-3T; *medium*, 4-6; *large*, 7-10)

MATERIALS

FABRIC A: ½ yd. of 44"-wide fabric like wool coating or tweed, velveteen*, or a lightweight felted sweater, for outside of hood

FABRIC B: ½ yd. of 44"-wide fabric like velveteen*, flannel, corduroy, or quilting cotton, for lining

1 yd. of ¼"- to ½"-wide ribbon

Coordinating thread

Hood pattern
(see Pattern Sheet 3; Pattern 12, five pieces: A-E)

*NOTE: Velveteen, or cotton velvet, is more difficult to work with than other recommended fabrics for this project, so if this is a first project for you, we recommend using wool or one of the other suggested fabrics.

1. Align and pin one cut ear and ear lining, with right sides together, and stitch the curved edge with a ½" seam. Trim the seam allowances to ⅛"; then turn the ear right side out, and finger-press the curved edge before pressing it with an iron.

2. Repeat Step 1 to prepare the second ear.

3. Fold each ear at the notch, so the right sides of the lining are touching. Baste the raw edges with a ⅜" seam to keep the ear folded.

4. Pin the two ears to the center hood, positioning them between the two upper placement notches, so the ears' fold is nearest the back of the hood and the ears open toward the front of the hood (see the illustration below). Baste the ears to the hood with a ⅜" seam.

ASSEMBLE THE HOOD

1. Align and pin one side-hood panel to the center hood, with right sides together, matching the raw edges and the notches and sandwiching the ear between the two layers. Clip into the seam allowances of the center hood to help it fit, if needed; then stitch the layers with a ½" seam.

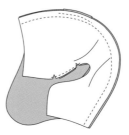

2. Pin and stitch the other side-hood panel to the center hood the same way. Then press the seam allowances open, and trim them to ¼".

3. Assemble the hood lining following steps 1-2 above, but leave an opening of about 3" near the back of one side seam for turning the hood right side out after sewing the lining to the hood. When you trim the seam allowances, don't trim the seam allowances at the opening left for turning.

4. Cut the ribbon into two equal ½-yard lengths, and pin one end of each length to the outside fabric at the notch on the flaps, as shown. Stitch the ribbon to the hood with a ⅜" seam, stitching back and forth across the ribbon several times to secure it and keep it from pulling out when the hood is worn. Then pin the remaining length of the ribbon to the hood on each side to keep it out of the way for the next steps.

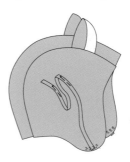

5. Turn the outside hood wrong side out and the lining right side out. Tuck the lining inside the hood (the hood and lining will be right sides together); and pin the two layers together, matching the raw edges, seams, and notches. Stitch the perimeter of the hood with a ½" seam.

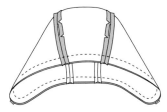

6. Trim the seam allowances to ¼" except where the ribbons are attached. Turn the hood right side out through the opening you left in the lining seam, and gently press the edge of the hood, rolling the seam slightly toward the inside.

FINISH THE HOOD

1. Use a blindstitch to close up the opening in the lining.

2. Open one ear, and finger-press it forward so that its fold line aligns with the hood's seam line. Take a few small hand stitches (or a bartack) across the ear at the base to encourage it to stand up and open a bit. If you stitch through the lining, your stitches will also help to hold the lining in place. Repeat with the second ear.

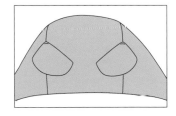

3. Dab a little fabric glue on the ends of the ribbons to prevent fraying.

messy kid bib

Every small child needs a really good bib. In designing this one, I combined my favorite elements from the many bibs we've used at home. It features an asymmetrical side opening that makes it easier to get on and off than a traditional bib with a back closure. It's cut wide across the chest and shoulders to keep even the messiest eaters clean. And it has a large front pocket that opens slightly to catch drips and spills before they end up on the furniture, the floor, or on a little one's lap.

For this project, I chose iron-on vinyl because it allows you to turn any printed cotton fabric into a waterproof surface that can be wiped clean with a damp cloth. If you haven't worked with this material before, you'll likely be amazed by what you can do with it.

SKILLS NEEDED

Applying bias binding

FINISHED SIZE

9¼" (from front neck) x 10½"

MATERIALS

NOTE: In dimensions throughout, length precedes width.

FABRIC A: 17" x 13" of lightweight fabric like quilting cotton, for bib front

FABRIC B: 17" x 13" of similar lightweight fabric, for bib back

FABRIC C: 12" x 8" of similar lightweight fabric, for bib pocket

24" of 17"-wide iron-on vinyl (see Resources on page 134)

3 yds. of ³⁄₈"-wide homemade bias binding (see page 126) or 1 package of ¼"-wide, double-folded, ready-made bias binding

Coordinating thread

1 sew-on snap or 1" of ¾"-wide Velcro

Masking or painter's tape

Tissue paper

Bib pattern (see Pattern Sheet 3; Pattern 13, two pieces: A-B)

1. Follow the manufacturer's instructions to iron the vinyl to the right side of Fabric A (for the bib front) and Fabric C (for the pocket) before cutting out the pattern pieces in the number and fabrics called for on the pattern pieces themselves.

NOTE: When sewing the vinyl-covered pattern pieces in the steps below, place a piece of tissue paper on the machine bed to keep the vinyl from sticking to the machine. You can easily tear the tissue away from the stitches afterwards.

MAKE THE POCKET

1. Align the two cut bib pockets, with wrong sides together, and baste the edges with a ¼" seam. Apply bias binding to the pocket's straight edge (see "Working with bias binding" on page 126). If you're using pins, be careful to pin only in the seam allowances so the pin holes won't show on the finished bib. Alternatively, you could use tape in place of pins.

ASSEMBLE THE BIB

1. Align and pin the front and back bib pieces, with wrong sides together, pinning only in the seam allowances. Then use a few pieces of tape to position the pocket on the bottom of the bib front's right side (note that the pocket is intentionally wider than the bib itself, so it will stand slightly away from the bib when worn). Finally baste the outer edge of the bib ¼" from the raw edges, catching the pocket's bottom edge in the stitching.

2. With the basted bib vinyl-side down under the needle (and with tissue paper under the vinyl on the machine bed), apply bias binding around the entire edge of the bib's back side, starting and ending the binding toward the bib's back-neck opening, so the join will be less visible. Then flip the bib to the front side, fold the binding over the edge to the front side, and edgestitch the binding in place to finish it.

FINISH THE BIB

1. Transfer the Velcro-placement markings from the bib (Pattern Piece 1) to the right side of the bib front, or just mark the center of each of these placement markings if you want to use a snap instead of Velcro.

2. Sew either the Velcro or snap in the marked position (if you're using Velcro, sew the soft part to the neckline on the bib's wrong side and the scratchy part to the neckline on the bib's right side).

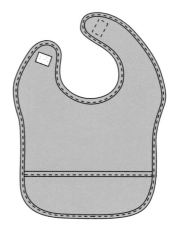

juggling balls and drawstring bag

Who doesn't love to watch a juggler? Following the paths the balls take as they move from hand to hand is mesmerizing for children as well as adults. But even better than watching someone juggle is learning to juggle yourself.

Juggling is a great activity for children. It improves gross and fine motor skills, helps develop self-confidence, and gives kids a cool trick that will impress their friends. Using the pattern provided, you can make juggling balls in two sizes—small for children up to age five and large for older children. If you want to create larger balls, enlarge the pattern as desired, making sure to add seam allowances to the stitching line. The bag will accommodate larger juggling balls— as long as you're enlarging within reason.

SKILLS NEEDED
Sewing curved seam, Edgestitching

FINISHED SIZES
SMALL JUGGLING BALL: 2 ½" diameter

LARGE JUGGLING BALL: 3" diameter

Drawstring bag: 12" x 11"

MATERIALS
NOTE: In dimensions throughout, length precedes width.

FOR ONE JUGGLING BALL: 6 fabric scraps, each at least 5" x 2", of quilting or other lightweight cotton

Cotton stuffing

Coordinating thread

Dried rice or beans, for weighting balls (optional)

FOR DRAWSTRING BAG: FABRIC A: ½ yd. of 44"-wide quilting cotton or other light- to medium-weight cotton, for bag's main panel and lining

FABRIC B: ¼ yd. of 44"-wide quilting cotton or other lightweight cotton, for bag's bottom and drawstring casing

1 ½ yds. of ¾"-wide twill tape

Coordinating thread

Bodkin or safety pin

Ball and Bag patterns (see Pattern Sheet 4; Pattern 17, six pieces: A-F)

JUGGLING BALLS

1. Pin two wedges together, with right sides facing and the edges and points aligned. Join the pinned edges with a ¼" seam, starting and stopping at the dots you transferred from the pattern piece and backstitching or lockstitching at the dots to secure your stitches.

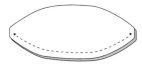

2. Open the two wedges, and pin a third wedge to one edge of the sewn pair, again with right sides together and matching the raw edges and points. Stitch the pinned edges with a ¼" seam, backstitching or lockstitching at the dots. These three wedges form one half-sphere. Make a second half-sphere repeating steps 1-2.

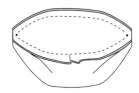

1. Turn one half-sphere right side out, and tuck it inside the other half-sphere turned wrong side out so that the right sides face together. Align the points and edges of the two half-spheres, and pin the edges together. Join the edges with a ¼" seam, stitching through the dots on the half-spheres (so each wedge will have a nice point on the finished ball) and leaving a 2" opening along one side for turning and stuffing the ball. Remember to backstitch or lockstitch at the beginning and end of your stitching.

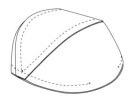

2. Turn the sphere right side out through the opening, and stuff it as firmly as you like. If you want to give the balls a little weight to make them more manageable for juggling, you might tuck a small fabric sack of dried beans or rice into the center of each ball. Then finger-press the seam allowances at the opening, and hand-stitch the opening closed with a blindstitch.

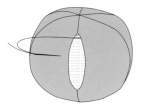

DRAWSTRING BAG

1. Align and pin one main panel and one bottom panel, with right sides together, and join them with a ½" seam. Press the seam allowances toward the bottom panel.

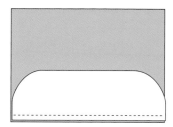

2. Trim the seam allowances at the outside edges to reduce bulk.

3. Edgestitch the bottom panel ⅛" from the seam, if you want.

HINT: Substituting a hand-sewn running stitch or a decorative embroidery stitch for the edgestitching would also be a nice touch here. If you want to embroider a name or another detail, now is the time to do it.

4. Assemble the second side of the bag, repeating steps 1-3 above.

SEW THE OUTSIDE BAG

1. With right sides together, align and pin the bag's two sides together at the outside edges, being careful to match the edges. Join the two layers with a ½" seam, beginning and ending at the dots you transferred from the pattern near the top of the bag, and backstitching or lockstitching at the beginning and end of the seam.

2. Press open the seam allowances at the side seams, evenly maintaining the seam allowances' width at the slits at the top edge. Trim the seam allowances at the curved bottom corners to approximately ⅛" (or clip the curves if you prefer); then turn the outside bag right side out. Finger-press the shape of the curves before pressing the bag with an iron.

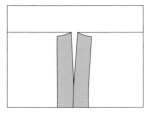

SEW THE BAG'S LINING

1. With right sides together, align and pin the two sides of the lining together at the side and bottom edges. Join the two layers with a ½" seam, beginning and ending at the dots you transferred from the pattern near the top of the bag, as you did with the outside of the bag, and backstitching or lockstitching at the beginning and end of the seam.

2. Press open the seam allowances at the sides, and trim the seam allowances at the curved bottom corners to about ⅛". Do not turn the bag right side out.

ASSEMBLE THE BAG

1. Slip the lining, still wrong side out, into the outside bag (the wrong sides of the lining and outside bag will face one another), and pin the two layers together, matching the raw top edges, side seams, and vents.

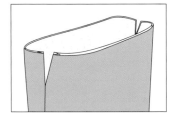

2. Baste the top edge of the bag and lining together with a ⅜" seam.

MAKE AND ATTACH THE CASINGS

1. Fold and press the short ends of one cut casing ½" to the wrong side. Fold and press one long edge of the casing ½" to the wrong side.

2. With right sides together, align and pin the casing's raw edge to the top edge of one side of the bag. Sew the casing to the bag with a ½" seam.

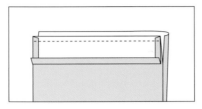

3. Press the seam allowances toward the casing; then trim the seam allowances to about ⅛".

4. Stitch the second casing to the other side of the bag repeating steps 1-3.

5. Edgestitch the end of the casing and the slit at the top of the bag, pivoting at the bottom of the slit to stitch across it and then pivoting again to stitch up the other side.

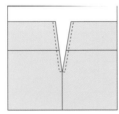

6. Fold and press the casings in half so that the folded edge covers the stitching at the bag's inside top edge.

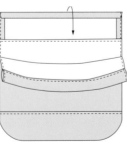

7. Working from the bag's right side, edgestitch the casing near the seam, catching the folded inside edge of the casing in the stitching.

8. Repeat steps 5-7 to complete the second casing on the other side of the bag.

FINISH THE BAG

1. Cut two pieces of twill tape, each 27" long.

2. Attach a safety pin or bodkin to one end of one length of twill tape. Starting at one side seam, feed the twill tape, safety-pinned end first, through both sides of the casing and back out to the side where you started.

3. Prepare the other length of twill tape as above, and feed it through the casings starting and ending at the opposite side.

4. Fold under all the cut ends of the twill tape by ½". Pin the folded ends of one twill-tape drawstring together, and stitch the pair with a small square or rectangle to form a pull-tab.

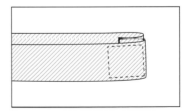

5. Repeat the process with the ends of the other drawstring. Pull both tabs simultaneously to close up the bag.

tea party doll dress

This little dress, designed for an 18" doll, is a miniature version of one of the first Oliver + S sewing patterns, the Tea Party Sundress. It has an interesting and unique silhouette, thanks to its flared skirt and curved bodice seam. The sewing instructions for this doll dress are easier and quicker than the instructions for the full-sized dress, but the finished product looks just as cute on a doll as the original does on a little girl.

ASSEMBLE THE DRESS FRONT AND BACK

1. Align and pin one side skirt panel to each side of one center skirt panel, with right sides together and matching the single notch on the pieces. Stitch the skirt panels together with a ¼" seam, backstitching or lockstitching at the beginning and end of the seams to secure your stitches. Assemble the remaining skirt pieces the same way, so you have a matching front and back skirt.

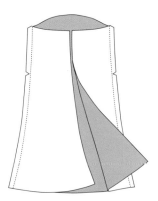

2. Press the seam allowances open, and finish them using your preferred method (see "Finish the seam allowances" in the Glossary on page 130).

3. Align and pin the front yoke to one skirt half, with right sides together, matching the notches on the bottom of the yoke with the skirt's seams. Take your time positioning and pinning these opposing curves, using plenty of pins to encourage the yoke to follow the shape of the skirt curve.

4. Once you're happy with how the yoke fits the curve of the skirt, stitch them together with a ¼" seam. Then press the seam allowances toward the yoke.

5. Follow steps 3-4 to assemble the back yoke and the other skirt half the same way.

6. Align and pin the front and back dress panels together at the side edges, with right sides together and matching the double notches. Stitch the sides with a ¼" seam. Press the seam allowances open, and finish them using your preferred method.

PREPARE AND ATTACH THE YOKE FACING

1. Align and pin the front and back yoke facings (the remaining cut front and back yokes), with right sides together and matching the side edges. Stitch the sides with a ¼" seam; then press the seam allowances open.

2. Finish the bottom edge of the facing, using your preferred method.

3. Turn the dress right side out, and slip the yoke facing, wrong side out, over the dress, so the right sides of the dress yoke and yoke facing face together. Align and pin the raw edges of the yoke and yoke facing, matching the side seams in the process. Then carefully stitch the facing to the dress with a ¼" seam, taking time to stitch the curves smoothly.

4. Trim the corners and clip the curves before turning the yoke right side out. Finger-press the edges before pressing them with an iron; then edgestitch the yoke to finish it.

5. Stitch the decorative buttons on the right side of the back yoke at the markings you transferred from the pattern. Then stitch one side of the snaps to the wrong side of the back yoke straps, under the buttons; and stitch the other side of the snap to the right side of the front yoke at the markings you transferred from the pattern, so that the back yoke straps overlap the front yoke.

HEM THE DRESS

1. Align and pin the two cut hem-facing pieces, with right sides together; and stitch the short sides with a ¼" seam. Press the seam allowances open.

2. Fold the top edge of the hem facing (the facing's inside curve) to the wrong side by ½", and press it.

3. Slip the hem facing over the dress, with rights sides together and the hems' raw edges aligned. Pin the two layers, matching the side seams, and stitch the hem facing to the dress with a ¼" seam.

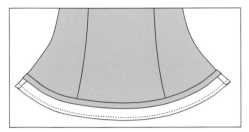

4. Press the hem facing away from the dress, and press the seam allowances toward the hem facing. Understitch (or edgestitch) the seam on the hem facing side, catching the seam allowances in your stitching. This understitching will force the hem-facing seam inside the dress, so it doesn't peek out when the hem is finished.

5. Turn the hem facing fully to the inside of the dress, and press it, rolling the facing's seam slightly to the inside of the skirt. Blindstitch the hem facing's top folded edge to the inside of the skirt to give the dress a clean finish. When finished, the hem facing will not show except on the inside of the dress, where this bit of Fabric A can be a little surprise.

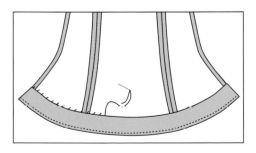

travel quilt

This simple quilt can be placed on the floor to provide a surface for a baby to play on, and it can be used as a lap quilt for cold morning rides in a car seat. Once the child is old enough to sleep with a blanket, it can also be used in a crib or on a toddler bed.

For this project, I wanted to create the illusion of two translucent layers of color overlapping each other to create a third color. A band of light blue, for example, overlaps a band of green, creating a small spot of turquoise. In a few places, I selected a polka-dotted or checked fabric to add a little more visual interest. If you want to make a quilt just like mine, see the fabric list on page 91. Or use your imagination to create your own unique quilt.

SKILLS NEEDED
Piecing patchwork, Machine- or hand-quilting, Applying bias binding

FINISHED SIZE
56 ½" x 39 ½"

MATERIALS
NOTE: In dimensions throughout, unless otherwise noted, length precedes width.

4 yds. of 44"-wide, white quilting cotton, for ground, binding, and quilt back (see page 91 for list of specific fabrics used in this quilt; also see "Make and attach the binding" section if you want to bind quilt with bias strips rather than straight-grain strips)

¼ yd. each of about 12 different quilting cottons in the following colors:

FABRICS A and R: large aqua dots

FABRICS B and G: light purple (could be same or different light purple fabrics)

FABRIC C: aqua checks

FABRIC D: light green

FABRICS E and K: light blue

FABRIC F: large yellow-green dots

FABRIC H: aqua dots

FABRICS I and O: medium green

FABRIC J: bright aqua

FABRIC L: pale green checks

FABRICS M and P: dark purple

FABRICS N and Q: dark blue-green

Coordinating thread

Lightweight, crib-sized quilt batting (we like Quilter's Dream; see Resources on page 134)

Water-soluble fabric-marking pen or chalk

Masking tape

Walking foot (recommended)

1. Audition combinations of fabric colors, and play with them before you start cutting. The goal is to create the illusion that two colors overlap to create a third color in the center, and you can use solids or prints to do this. We used mostly solids, but if you want to use prints, step back and squint at the prints when evaluating them to see each one's overall color.

CUT THE WHITE FABRIC

I think it's easiest to cut all the white fabric before cutting the various colored strips and suggest organizing your cutting as follows:

1. For the quilt back: Cut a 60" length of fabric using the fabric's full selvedge-to-selvedge width, and set it aside.

2. For the quilt-front strips: Cut the strips listed below (note that, in the cutting dimensions for these quilt-front strips, the width precedes the length). To avoid confusion later, write each strip's number on a scrap of paper and pin the paper to the strip to identify it, or write directly on the fabric with a water-soluble fabric-marking pen or chalk.

S1: Two strips 39 ½" x 5"
S2: Five strips 39 ½" x 4 ½"
S3: One strip 21 ½" x 2"
S4: One strip 12 ½" x 2"
S5: Two strips 18 ½" x 2"
S6: Two strips 15 ½" x 2"
S7: Two strips 15 ½" x 2"
S8: Two strips 18 ½" x 2"
S9: One strip 12 ½" x 2"
S10: One strip 21 ½" x 2"

3. For the binding: Cut five strips, 2 ½" long using the fabric's full selvedge-to-selvedge width, and set these strips aside.

CUT THE COLORED STRIPS

Once you've determined which color will go where on your quilt, you can start cutting the colored strips (note that, in the cutting dimensions for these colored strips, the width precedes the length). Label each cut strip (A1, A2, B1, B2, etc.) by noting on a piece of paper the strip's number and dimensions and pinning the paper to strip, or by writing on the strip with a water-soluble fabric-marking pen or chalk.

FABRIC A — A1: 18 ½" x 2", **A2:** 12 ½" x 2"
FABRIC B — B1: 21 ½" x 2", **B2:** 27 ½" x 2"
FABRIC C — C1: 21 ½" x 2", **C2:** 15 ½" x 2"
FABRIC D — D1: 18 ½" x 2", **D2:** 24 ½" x 2"
FABRIC E — E1: 24 ½" x 2", **E2:** 18 ½" x 2"
FABRIC F — F1: 15 ½" x 2", **F2:** 21 ½" x 2"
FABRIC G — G1: 27 ½" x 2", **G2:** 21 ½" x 2"
FABRIC H — H1: 12 ½" x 2", **H2:** 18 ½" x 2"
FABRIC I — I1: 24 ½" x 2", **I2:** 18 ½" x 2"
FABRIC J — J1: 15 ½" x 2", **J2:** 21 ½" x 2"
FABRIC K — K1: 21 ½" x 2", **K2:** 15 ½" x 2"
FABRIC L — L1: 18 ½" x 2", **L2:** 24 ½" x 2"
FABRICS M — M1: 6 ½" x 2"
FABRIC N — N1: 6 ½" x 2"
FABRIC O — O1: 6 ½" x 2"
FABRIC P — P1: 6 ½" x 2"
FABRIC Q — Q1: 6 ½" x 2"
FABRIC R — R1: 6 ½" x 2"

PIECE THE HORIZONTAL STRIPS

1. Follow the piecing diagram at right to assemble each of the quilt's pieced strips (for example, stitch A1 to S3 to assemble the first pieced strip), as follows: Align and pin the short ends of the pieces to be joined, with right sides together, and stitch them with a ¼" seam. I like to assemble one strip at a time, but you can use any piecing method you like. Be sure to keep the pieces in order as you assemble them, and always use a ¼" seam to join them.

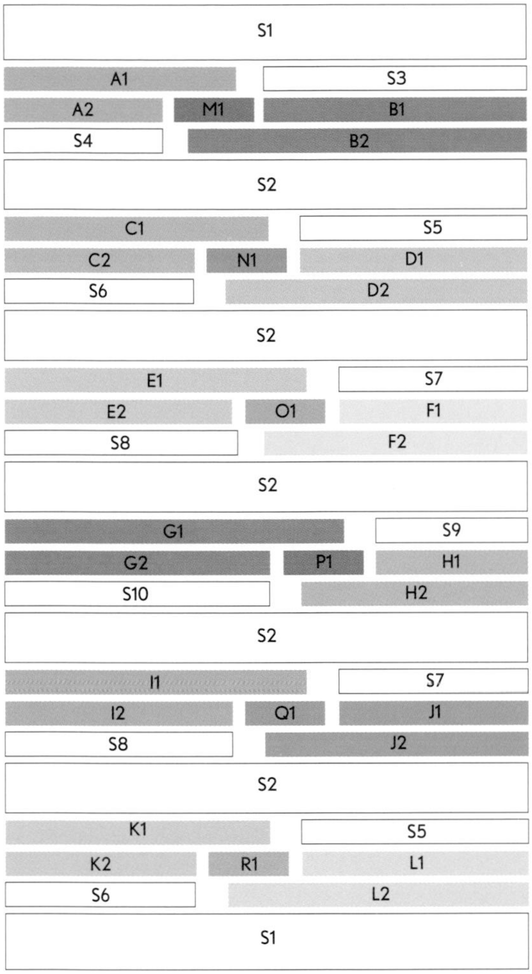

Diagram (left column):

- S1
- A1 | S3
- A2 | M1 | B1
- S4 | B2
- S2
- C1 | S5
- C2 | N1 | D1
- S6 | D2
- S2
- E1 | S7
- E2 | O1 | F1
- S8 | F2
- S2
- G1 | S9
- G2 | P1 | H1
- S10 | H2
- S2
- I1 | S7
- I2 | Q1 | J1
- S8 | J2
- S2
- K1 | S5
- K2 | R1 | L1
- S6 | L2
- S1

2. For strips with three pieces, press the seam allowances toward the ends of the strips. For strips with two pieces, press the seam allowances toward the colored side of the strip, which will prevent the seam allowances from showing through the white fabric and will help to "lock" the seams together when you start joining strips in the next step.

After sewing and pressing all the horizontal strips, you can assemble the quilt top, which I suggest doing in groups, as explained in detail in the steps below. In short, you'll assemble the three colored-fabric strips in each group first and then attach an S2 white strip to the bottom edge of each colored group except for the bottom group. For the bottom group, you'll sew an S1 white strip to its bottom edge, then attach an S1 white strip to the top edge of the first color group, as shown in the diagram. Finally you'll join each group to its neighboring group.

1. Align and pin the long edges of two corresponding strips (refer to the diagram to be sure to arrange the strips properly), with right sides together. As you pin, be sure to match the short ends and, where applicable, the pieced seams. Because you've pressed the seam allowances on each strip in opposite directions, the seams will "lock" when you align them, helping to create perfect points.

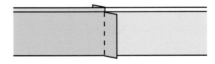

2. Join the pinned strips with a ¼" seam, and press the seam allowances open.

CREATE THE QUILT SANDWICH

1. Press the quilt top and backing. Lay the backing, right side down, on a large, flat, clean surface; and smooth the fabric so it lies completely flat. Tape the edges (but not the corners) to the surface with masking tape to hold the fabric in place.

2. Center the batting on the backing, and smooth it out flat.

3. Lay the quilt top over the batting, right side up, making sure that the top and backing are aligned, and smooth the quilt top over the batting and the backing.

4. Pin or baste the layers together to secure them until you've quilted them together. I prefer to use safety pins for this step, but some people like to hand-baste the layers in place. Baste or pin the layers, beginning at the center of the quilt and working out toward the edges.

QUILT THE LAYERS

Hand-quilting is really beautiful and enjoyable to do if you have the time. To hand-quilt, thread a small needle with about 18" of hand-quilting thread. Beginning at the center of the quilt, push the needle down through the quilt top into the batting. Tug the thread slightly, so the knot pops through the quilt top and lodges in the batting, which will make the knot invisible.

Then you can quilt with a short running stitch, about six stitches per inch. When you have just a few inches of thread left, make a knot close to the fabric, push the needle back into the quilt top and batting, and come back up through the top about ½" from where you entered the quilt. Pull the needle and thread quickly and somewhat forcefully, so the knot pops underneath the quilt top and lodges in the batting.

To machine-quilt, as we did with the sample in the photograph, you'll need to replace your presser foot on your sewing machine with a walking foot to keep the layers smooth and even as you stitch. Start in the center of the quilt, and work your way out toward the edges. For this design, I quilted with straight lines about ¼" from the seams themselves, using white cotton thread on the white ground and coordinating colored thread on the colored strips. You can use

any quilting pattern you like, and different patterns can give the quilt a very different finished appearance. Note that the sample quilt in the photograph is machine-quilted with horizontal lines mimicking its piecing, but, for clarity's sake, the quilting in the drawings on page 90 is rendered as diamond quilting.

Once you've finished quilting, trim the excess batting and backing from the quilt so that these layers match the dimensions of the quilt top.

MAKE AND ATTACH THE BINDING

The binding for this quilt is made with straight-grain strips, but you could also bind the quilt with bias strips, as explained in "Working with bias binding" on page 126. Note that, if you want to use bias strips, you'll need to increase the white fabric yardage called for in the Materials list to 5 yards total.

1. Trim the selvedges from the ends of the five cut binding strips, and join the strips into one long strip by positioning the ends of the strips perpendicular to each other, with right sides together. Stitch diagonally across the strips from outside corner to outside corner, as shown in the illustration, backstitching at both ends; and trim the seam allowances to ¼".

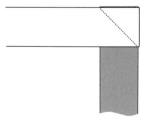

2. Press the seam allowances open, and trim any corners that extend beyond the strip's edges (if you stitched the strips together from corner to corner, you probably won't have any corners extending). Continue to join the strips until all five strips are assembled.

3. Fold the binding in half along its length, with wrong sides together, and lightly press the fold.

4. With the quilt right side up, start pinning the raw edges of the binding (you're handling the two layers of the binding as a single layer) to the raw edge of the quilt front, beginning in the center of one side of the quilt. Begin stitching the binding to the quilt with a ¼" seam, starting 5" to 6" from the end of the binding (which will give you room to join the binding's two ends when you return to your starting point). When you near the first corner, stop, and then backstitch ¼" from the corner edge. Then take the binding out from under the needle, and cut the thread so that you can reposition the quilt and binding as described in the next step.

5. To miter the corner, fold the binding perpendicular to the quilt's sewn edge, away from the quilt itself. Then fold the binding back onto itself so that its raw edge is even with the quilt's next raw edge. Pin the binding in place; then begin stitching it with a ¼" seam again, starting at the edge of the quilt (remember to backstitch at both ends of your stitching).

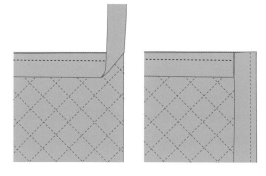

6. Continue repeating steps 4-5 until you're about 12" from where you began attaching the binding.

7. To join the two ends of the binding, unfold the remaining binding, and form a 45-degree angle in the center of the remaining unsewn quilt edge, as shown. Crease the folds where they meet.

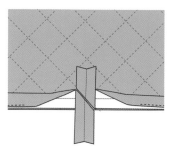

8. Unfold the two creased folds; and, with right sides together, align and pin just the creased fold lines to each other, so the two strips are at a right angle to each other, just as they were when you joined the five binding strips together in Step 1 above.

9. Check to be sure the length of the pinned binding equals the length of the remaining quilt edge so that the binding will lie flat along the edge, and adjust the strip's pinned fold lines if necessary. Then stitch the matched and pinned fold lines, creating a diagonal seam.

10. Trim the seam allowances to ¼", and press them open. Re-fold the binding in half, and finish stitching the binding to the quilt.

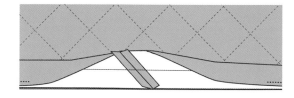

11. Turn the quilt to the back, and fold the binding over the quilt's raw edges. Blind stitch the binding's folded edge so that it covers the stitching line attaching the binding to the quilt front.

FABRICS USED FOR
TRAVEL QUILT

GROUND, BINDING, AND BACKING FABRIC:
Robert Kaufman Kona Cotton snow 1339

FABRICS A AND R: Lecien Color Basic
4506 CM

FABRICS B AND G: Robert Kaufman Kona
Cotton grape mist 318

FABRIC C: Custom-designed Blue Grid,
printing courtesy of Spoonflower

FABRIC D: P&B Textiles Color Spectrum mint
CSPE 02G

FABRICS E AND K: Robert Kaufman Kona
Cotton aqua 1005

FABRIC F: Lecien Color Basic 4506 CG

FABRIC H: Custom-designed Blue Dot,
printing courtesy of Spoonflower

FABRICS I AND O: Robert Kaufman Kona
Cotton pistachio 1293

FABRIC J: P&B Textiles Color Spectrum sky
CSPE 02BG

FABRIC L: Custom-designed Green Grid,
printing courtesy of Spoonflower

FABRICS M AND P: Robert Kaufman Kona
Cotton lavender 1189

FABRICS N AND Q: Robert Kaufman Kona
Cotton candy green 1061

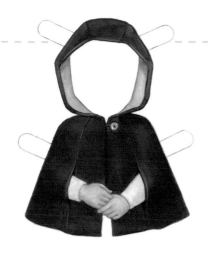

red riding hood

I've yet to meet a girl who doesn't love this Red Riding Hood cape. In red, it is a perfect accessory for fairytale play, but it can, of course, be made in any color. If made in warm wool or fleece fabric, it works perfectly as a feminine, cool-weather cover-up.

Have fun choosing the lining. I used a colorful, large-scale print for the cape shown here, but just about any print or solid will work. Perhaps your little girl will enjoy choosing the lining herself.

SKILLS NEEDED

Sewing curved seam, Edgestitching

FINISHED SIZES

Medium, fits up to size 4 (*large*, sizes 5-10)

Length from shoulder seam at neckline, 16 ¾" (21 ½")

MATERIALS

FABRIC A: 1½ yds. (2 yds.) of 44"-wide, light- to heavy-weight fabric like quilting or home-dec-weight cotton, linen, corduroy, wool melton, or wool coating, for outside of cape

FABRIC B: 1½ yds. (2 yds.) of 44"-wide, lightweight fabric like quilting cotton, for cape lining

3" length of ¼"-wide ribbon, for button loop (optional)

Coordinating thread

One ¾" button

Knitting needle or chopstick

Cape pattern (see Pattern Sheet 4; Pattern 18, seven pieces: A-G) and cutting diagram on page 125

1. Working with both the cut Fabric A and Fabric B pattern pieces, staystitch the arm opening (between the dots) on each front panel and front-side panel, and staystitch the shoulder edge of each front- and back-side panel with a ⅜" seam. (The staystitching will not be shown in the illustrations.)

ASSEMBLE THE FRONT, BACK, AND LINING

1. Working with the cut Fabric A pieces, align and pin one front panel and one front-side panel, with right sides together, matching the raw edges and the dots for the arm opening. Stitch the two pieces together, backstitching at the beginning and end of the seams and stopping at the dots. Leave the section between the dots unsewn.

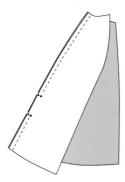

2. Press the seam allowances open.

3. Repeat steps 1-2 to assemble the second front half of the cape.

4. Align and pin the cut Fabric A back-side panels to the back panel, with right sides together, matching the raw edges and notches as you did for the front panels. Stitch the full length of the panels with a ½" seam, backstitching or lockstitching at the beginning and end of the seam.

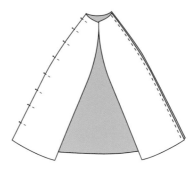

5. Press the seam allowances open.

6. Working with the cut Fabric B pieces, repeat steps 1-5 to assemble the cape lining, changing thread colors, if necessary, to match Fabric B.

JOIN THE FRONT AND BACK OF THE CAPE

1. Align and pin the two Fabric A front halves of the cape to the back of the cape, with right sides together, matching the raw edges. Stitch the side seams with a ½" seam. Press the seam allowances open, clipping the allowances as needed along the curves to help them lie flat when pressed open.

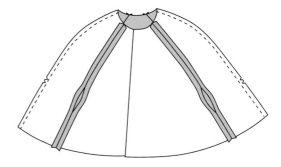

2. Repeat Step 1 to assemble the Fabric B front halves and back of the cape lining, again changing thread colors, if necessary, to match Fabric B.

1. Working with the cut Fabric A pieces, align and pin one side hood to the center hood, with right sides together, matching the single and double notches. Clip into the center hood's seam allowance to make it fit the curve of the side hood, if necessary, being careful not to clip into the seam line itself. Then stitch the two pieces together with a ½" seam, and press the seam allowances open.

2. Repeat Step 1 to attach the second side of the outside hood. Then repeat steps 1-2 to assemble the hood lining.

3. Turn the hood lining right side out, and pin it to the outside hood, so the right sides face together, matching the seams, raw edges, and notches. Stitch the outside edge of the hood with a ½" seam, leaving the neck edge unstitched.

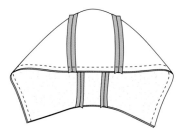

4. Trim the seam allowances to ¼", and turn the hood right side out through the neck opening. Finger-press the outside edge of the hood, rolling the seam slightly toward the inside to keep it from showing, and then press the edge with an iron.

5. Pin and baste the hood and hood lining together at the neck edge with a ⅜" seam.

NOTE: If you're making the button loop from ribbon rather than cut fabric, jump to Step 4 below.

1. Fold the button loop in half lengthwise, with wrong sides together, and press the crease to create a center fold line.

2. Open the button loop, and lay it flat and wrong side up. Fold each long raw edge in toward the center, and press the folds. Fold the loop in half again (along the center line formed in Step 1) and press it, enclosing the raw edges in the fold. The button loop is now folded into four fabric thicknesses.

3. Edgestitch the folded button loop along the long, open edge and trim the loop to be 3" long.

4. Fold the loop in half lengthwise (to make the actual loop), and pin the two ends to the notch near the neckline on the cape's center front edge on what will be the wearer's right side. Baste the loop in place with a ⅜" seam.

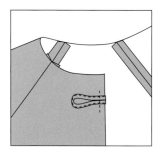

1. Pin the hood to the outside cape, with right sides together, matching the notches at the front cape's neckline with the hood's front edges and the notches on the hood's neckline with the cape's shoulder seams. Baste the hood to the cape with a $\frac{3}{8}$" seam.

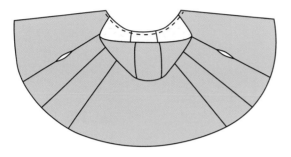

2. Align and pin the cape and the cape lining, with right sides together, sandwiching the hood between the two pieces. Match and pin the entire circumference of the cape—the neckline, front edges, and hem. Stitch the cape and cape lining together with a $\frac{1}{2}$" seam, pivoting at the corners.

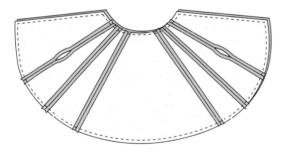

3. Trim the seam allowances to $\frac{1}{4}$", and clip the corners. Then turn the entire cape right side out through one of the armhole openings.

4. Gently push out the corners of the cape with a knitting needle or chopstick; then finger-press the edges before pressing them with an iron, gently rolling the seams slightly to the inside to give the cape a neat, finished appearance.

1. Pin the arm openings of the cape and the cape lining together, so the folded edges and ends of the openings match. Then edgestitch the layers together with a rectangle, pivoting to stitch the circumference of the opening, or slipstitch the opening together by hand to give it a finished appearance.

2. Sew a button on the wearer's left-hand side of the cape at the mark you transferred from the pattern. Note that the two front edges should overlap each other by $\frac{1}{2}$", so the edges of the hood do not meet at center front.

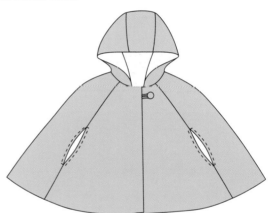

explorer vest

Children are natural explorers and collectors, and they tend to adore garments with pockets for the treasures they gather—from action figures and marbles, to acorns, leaves, and sticks. This vest boasts five pockets, enough for even the most impassioned trinket hoarder. Make the vest with simple patch pockets, as shown in the photos, or the pocket bellows to expand their capacity and give the vest even more of an explorer feeling.

SKILLS NEEDED

Applying bias binding, Sewing on button and buttonhole (optional), Sewing curved seam, Topstitching

FINISHED SIZES

Small, fits up to size 3 (*medium*, sizes 4-6; *large*, sizes 7-10)

Chest, 25 ½" (28 ½", 30 ½")

Length from shoulder seam at neckline, 13 ¾" (16 ¼", 18 ⅝")

MATERIALS

FABRIC A: ¾ yd. (1 yd., 1 yd.) of 44"-wide, light- to medium-weight woven fabric like quilting cotton, home-dec-weight fabric, lightweight canvas or denim, or cotton twill (avoid heavy fabrics), for vest and pockets

FABRIC B: ½ yd. (½ yd., ¾ yd.) of 44"-wide, lightweight fabric like quilting cotton, for lining

Two 20" (22", 24") lengths of ½"-wide homemade bias binding (see page 126) or 1 package of ½"-wide, double-folded, ready-made bias binding

Coordinating thread

3 buttons, snaps, or sew-on Velcro squares, for center-front closure

Knitting needle or chopstick

Vest pattern (see Pattern Sheet 1; Pattern 5, nine pieces: A-I) and cutting diagram on page 125

1. To hem the pocket, fold and press the top edge of one pocket to the wrong side by ½". Then fold the top edge again, this time to the right side by ¾", and pin it in place. Stitch the side edges of the pocket at the folds with a ½" seam.

2. Turn the resulting hem of the pocket to the right side, gently pushing out the corners with a chopstick or knitting needle, and press it. Fold the remaining side edges toward the wrong side by ½", and press them. Fold the bottom edge toward the wrong side by ½", and press it.

3. Edgestitch the pocket hem at the top edge at the innermost folded edge.

4. Pin the pocket to the front of the vest at the placement markings you transferred from the pattern, and edgestitch it in place, backstitching or lockstitching at the beginning and end of the seam and pivoting at the corners.

FRONT AND BACK BELLOWS POCKETS (MORE DIFFICULT VERSION)

1. Fold and press one long edge of the back pocket bellows to the wrong side by ½". Then align and pin the bellows' opposite long edge to the back pocket's outside edge, with right sides together and matching the center notches and the raw edges. Carefully clip into the seam allowances of the bellows at the curves, to help it fit the pocket. Stitch the bellows to the pocket with a ½" seam.

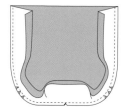

2. Trim the stitched seam allowances to ⅛", and press them to one side (either side will do). Then fold and press the top edge of the pocket and bellows to the wrong side twice: first by ½", then by ¾". Edgestitch the innermost fold to hem the pocket.

3. Fold the pocket and bellows together at the perimeter, so the wrong sides face together; then edgestitch the pocket's perimeter to help give the pocket definition and a finished appearance.

4. Pin the folded edges of the bellows to the vest back at the placement markings you transferred from the pattern. Then edgestitch the bellows to the vest back, backstitching or lockstitching at the beginning and end of the seam.

5. Pin the top corners of the pocket to cover the bellows, forming a little pleat in the bellows at the top edge. Bartack the pocket to the bellows and the vest at the pocket's top side edges for about ½", stitching over the edgestitching added in Step 3 above.

6. Repeat steps 1-5 to make and attach the two front bellows pockets to the vest.

FRONT AND BACK PATCH POCKETS (SIMPLER VERSION)

1. Run a basting stitch around the curved edge of the back pocket, ½" from the outside edge. This basting will be used as the fold line for the patch pockets.

2. Hem the pocket the same way that you did for the chest pockets for the vest: Fold and press the top edge of the pocket to the wrong side by ½". Then fold the top edge again, this time to the right side by ¾", and pin it in place. Stitch the side edges of the pocket at the folds with a ½" seam.

3. Trim the seam allowances (including the basted outside edge of the pocket) to ¼" to reduce bulk, if you want, before turning and pressing the pocket's hem to the right side, gently pushing out the corners with a chopstick or knitting needle.

4. Fold and press the pocket's outside edges toward the wrong side, using the basting stitches from Step 1 as a folding guide.

5. Edgestitch the pocket hem at the innermost folded edge.

6. Pin the pocket to the vest back at the placement markings you transferred from the pattern, and edgestitch it in place, backstitching or lockstitching at the beginning and end of the seam, and taking care when sewing the curves.

7. Repeat steps 1-6 to make and attach the two front pockets to the vest.

SEW THE POCKET FLAPS

1. Align and pin the two back pocket flap pieces together with right sides facing, and stitch the curved edge with a ½" seam. Leave the top (straight) edge open for turning the flap right side out.

2. Trim the seam allowances to ⅛", and turn the flap right side out, finger-pressing the edges before pressing them with an iron. Edgestitch the sewn edge.

3. Pin the pocket flap to the vest, so the flap's raw edge meets the hem of the back pocket. Stitch the flap to the vest with a ¼" seam.

4. Trim the seam allowance to a scant ⅛"; then press the flap over the seam allowance, and stitch the flap again, this time with a generous ⅛" seam. The seam allowances will be sandwiched in the seam, so the flap will have a clean finish. Take care to keep from stitching the top of the pocket closed in this step.

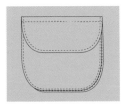

5. Repeat steps 1-4 to assemble and attach the two front pocket flaps the same way.

ASSEMBLE THE VEST

1. Align and pin the two front vest pieces to the back vest, with right sides together, matching the shoulders and the sides. Stitch the shoulders and sides with a ½" seam, backstitching or lockstitching at the beginning and end of the seams.

2. Trim the seam allowances to ¼", and press them open.

3. Repeat steps 1-2 to assemble the vest lining.

4. Turn the vest wrong side out, and pin the vest to the lining, with right sides together, matching the edges and seams. Stitch the perimeter of the vest—the neckline, front edge, and hem—in one continuous seam, pivoting at the corners and backstitching when you arrive back at your starting point. Do not stitch the armholes.

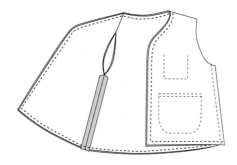

5. Trim the seam allowances to ⅛", and clip the corners and curves. Then turn the vest right side out through one of the armholes. Finger-press the edges, rolling the seam slightly to the inside. Use a chopstick or knitting needle to gently push out the corners; then press the edges with an iron.

6. Edgestitch the perimeter of the vest to give it a neat appearance.

FINISH THE VEST

1. Prepare two strips of bias binding about 20" (22", 24") x 2" (see "Working with bias binding" on page 126 for detailed information on making and attaching this binding), and fold and press the strips in preparation for applying them.

2. Pin the vest and lining together at the armholes, matching the raw edges and seams; and baste the pair together with a ⅜" seam. Then apply the bias binding to the armholes, beginning on the lining side of the vest. Position the beginning and end of the binding near the bottom of the armhole, so the join is less visible when the vest is worn.

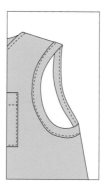

3. Stitch the buttonholes on the wearer's left side and the buttons on the right, using the markings you transferred from the pattern. If you prefer, you can use Velcro or snaps in place of the buttons.

bear carrier

My daughter and husband usually visit a museum or art gallery on Saturdays. Often my daughter carries a sketchbook with her, but sometimes she likes to take Bear, her favorite stuffed animal, instead. It was after she invented a rubber-band-around-the-neck "baby carrier" for Bear that I had the idea to make this child-sized doll carrier.

The carrier fits dolls ranging from 9" to 18" tall and can be adjusted to fit children from about three to eight years old. It's not a difficult project to complete, but it does require sewing a number of curves. If you're new to curves, take them slowly, and don't be afraid to hand-crank your sewing machine so that you can adjust the fabric every few stitches. You'll still be surprised at how quickly and easily the carrier comes together.

SKILLS NEEDED

Sewing button and buttonhole, Sewing curved seam, Topstitching

FINISHED SIZE

Fits most bears or dolls 9" to 18" tall; can be worn by children aged 3 to 8

MATERIALS

NOTE: In dimensions throughout, length precedes width.

FABRIC A: 14" x 12" of light- to medium-weight fabric like quilting cotton, home-dec-weight fabric, canvas, denim, or cotton twill, for outside of carrier

FABRIC B: 14" x 12" of quilting cotton, for carrier lining

FABRIC C: ⅓ yd. of 44"-wide, home-dec-weight or quilting cotton, for carrier straps

14" x 12" of lightweight quilt batting (see Resources on page 134)

Two or four ⅞"-1" buttons

Two or four 1" Velcro squares or circles

Coordinating thread

Knitting needle or chopstick

Walking foot (recommended)

Carrier pattern (see Pattern Sheet 2; Pattern 10, three pieces: A-C), plus two 42" x 5" rectangles from Fabric C (no pattern piece included for straps)

SEW AND ATTACH THE POCKET

1. With the fabrics' right sides together and their top edges aligned, stitch the top edge of the pocket lining to the top edge of the pocket with a ½" seam.

2. Press the stitched seam allowances toward the lining, and trim them to ⅛" near the pocket's side edges to reduce bulk when sewing the pocket's perimeter in the next step.

3. Re-fold the pocket and lining in half at the notches, with right sides together; and pin the two together, matching the raw edges. Stitch the perimeter of the pocket with a ½" seam, leaving an opening at the bottom between the dots you transferred from the pattern piece for turning the pocket right side out.

> **HINT:** When leaving an opening for turning the pocket right side out, start and end your stitching at the raw edge of the seam allowance, as shown in the illustration above, pivoting when you reach the seam line. By sewing across the seam allowances, they'll be forced inside the opening when you turn the pocket right side out.

4. Trim the seam allowances (except for those along the opening) to about ⅛"; then turn the pocket right side out, using a knitting needle or chopstick to gently but fully turn out the corners. Finger-press the pocket's edges, tuck the seam allowances inside the opening, and press the pocket with an iron.

5. Pin the pocket on the Fabric A front of the carrier at the pocket-placement markings you transferred from the pattern. Edgestitch the pocket's sides and bottom curves to the carrier (which will also close the opening left at the bottom of the pocket for turning it right side out), backstitching at the beginning and end of your stitching.

MAKE THE STRAPS

1. Cut two 42" x 5" strips from Fabric C for the carrier's straps. Fold one strap in half lengthwise, with wrong sides together, and press the crease to create a center-fold line.

2. Open the strap, and lay it flat and wrong side up. Fold each long raw edge in toward the center-fold line, and press the folds.

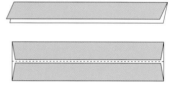

3. Fold the strap in half again along the center-fold line, and press it, enclosing its raw edges in the fold. The strap is now folded into four fabric thicknesses.

4. Edgestitch the strap near the long open edge, and again along the opposite folded edge to finish the strap. Repeat steps 1-4 to make the second strap.

ASSEMBLE THE CARRIER

1. Sew a line of basting stitches ½" from the top edge of the Fabric A main panel between the dots you transferred from the pattern (the basting will become a folding guide later when you finish the carrier). Baste the Fabric B lining panel the same way.

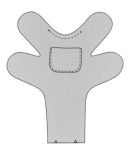

2. Pin the two straps between the notches at the lower edge of the main panel, angling the straps slightly toward the panel's outer edges. Baste the straps to the main panel at the bottom edge with a ³⁄₈" seam.

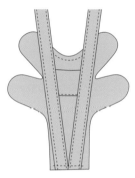

3. Pin the straps together so that they extend beyond the main panel only between the dots at the top of the panel (to prevent them from getting caught in the stitching when you sew the three layers together in the next step).

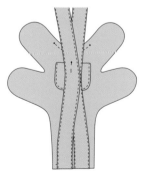

4. Create a sandwich of the carrier's three layers as follows: Place the quilt batting layer down first, align

the fabric panel right side up atop the batting, and align the lining panel wrong side up on top (the right sides of the two fabrics should face one another). Pin the three layers together, and use your walking foot (if available) to stitch the perimeter starting at one dot at the top of the carrier and stitching around the outside edge, taking your time with the many curves. Rotate the carrier at the corners to stitch across the bottom edge, and end your stitching at the other dot. You'll be leaving an opening where the straps extend and where you basted in Step 1 above.

> **HINT:** Use your sewing machine needle to help you stitch the curves by dropping your needle in the fabric and picking up the presser foot between stitches so that you can rotate the fabric slightly. You can use this technique with every stitch on the really tight curves or as the need arises when the curve is more gradual. Take your time, and you'll stitch neat, even curves.

5. Trim the seam allowances to ¹⁄₈" except for the fabric layers along the top opening (at the opening, just trim the batting).

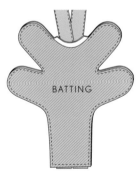

BATTING

6. Turn the carrier right side out through the opening, using a knitting needle or chopstick to gently push out each curve. Finger-press the curves; then press the carrier flat with an iron.

7. Tuck the unsewn edges inside the opening, clipping into the seam allowances as needed to help them turn in and lie flat. Use your basting stitches as a folding guide for the carrier's outside edge, wrapping the front fabric (Fabric A) around the batting to cover it before you pin the folded edges together. Hand-stitch the opening closed with a blindstitch, or simply edgestitch around the entire carrier to simultaneously close the opening and give the carrier a finished appearance.

8. Stitch the buttonholes at the markings you transferred from the pattern.

FINISH THE CARRIER

1. Turn the carrier to the lining side, and sew the buttons to the straps, using the following measurements as guidelines: For a small bear or doll (9" to 12" tall), stitch the buttons to the straps about 4" from the bottom of the carrier; for a medium- to large-sized bear or doll (13" to 18" tall), position the buttons about 8" from the bottom (before stitching the buttons, place the bear/doll in the carrier to check the button placement). To make the carrier adjustable for various sizes of bears and dolls, use both sets of buttons.

2. Sew the scratchy part of two Velcro squares or circles to the lining side of the carrier on the side tab, using the markings you transferred from the pattern.

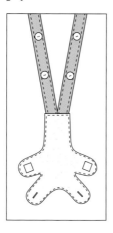

3. To determine the position for the soft part of the Velcro squares or circles, place the carrier wrong side up, as shown in the illustration at left, and position the bear on its back on top of the carrier, so its legs straddle the narrowest part of the carrier. Wrap the carrier up over the bear, positioning the buttonhole tabs over its shoulders and the Velcro tabs around its waist, and button the bear into the carrier. Then position the carrier at the child's front, with the straps over the child's shoulders. When the bear is in a comfortable position for the child, cross the straps behind the child, and mark the placement of the Velcro where the straps join the side tabs. Additional pieces of Velcro can be sewn to the straps to make the carrier adjustable for different-sized bears or dolls as the child grows. Stitch the soft part of the Velcro squares or circles to the straps. When the carrier is worn, the ends of the straps can be tucked into the carrier behind the bear or doll.

4. Trim the straps to the desired length and finish the ends with any method you prefer. For a clean finish, remove 1"-2" of edgestitching at each strap's end and fold the strap's raw ends inside the strap before re-folding and re-stitching the strap's edges and end. Alternatively you can simply satin-stitch the straps' ends for an easy finish.

bear puppet bath mitt

This puppet wash mitt is quick and simple to sew and
is easy to personalize with embellishments, such as an
embroidered bow tie or buttons down the front to suggest
a shirt. I made the mitt shown here in terry cloth so that it
could be used in the bathtub, but if you're not planning to
subject your mitt to water (for example, if you're planning
to use it with the Puppet Theater on page 112), you could
choose wool, felt, or corduroy.

DESIGN OPTIONS

If you want to make this bath mitt as a play puppet to accompany the Puppet Theater on page 112, you might try using corduroy, wool coating, or wool felt for the body. You could also line the puppet by cutting and stitching together a second pair of the body pieces cut from a lightweight cotton fabric and tucking it into the sewn puppet before hemming it. Of course, a puppet might get a button nose and eyes instead of an embroidered face—in short, have fun embellishing and changing this basic pattern to suit your preferences.

ATTACH THE SNOUT

1. Draw or trace the shape of the snout pattern on the paper liner of the fusible web. Then follow the manufacturer's directions to fuse the web to the wrong side of the snout fabric.

2. Cut the fabric and the fusible web along the traced oval line. Then peel the liner from the web, leaving the web on the fabric itself.

3. Position the snout on the right side of the fabric (use the pattern piece as a template for placement, if you want); and once you're happy with the placement, follow the manufacturer's directions to fuse the snout to the fabric.

4. Satin-stitch by machine around the snout's raw edge. You may find it helpful to stop stitching occasionally, with your needle down in the fabric; lift your presser foot; and maneuver the fabric as needed to continue sewing (remember to lower the presser foot before stitching again).

EMBROIDER THE FACE

1. Use your iron-on transfer pencil to trace the eyes, nose, and mouth from the body pattern's face template on the back of the traced pattern piece; and

follow the manufacturer's directions to transfer the markings onto the right side of the bear's face.

2. Embroider the bear's eyes, nose, and mouth. We used a hand-embroidered satin stitch for the eyes and nose, and a backstitch for the mouth (see facing page).

MAKE THE EARS

1. Align and pin two ear pieces, with right sides together. Stitch the curved outside edge with a ½" seam, starting and ending at the fabric's outside raw edges and pivoting at the dots you transferred from the pattern.

> **HINT:** If you're using a stretchy fabric (like terry cloth), you might find it helpful to fuse lightweight interfacing to one of the ear pieces so that the ear keep its shape as you stitch.

2. Trim the seam allowances (except at the opening) to ¼". Turn the ear right side out through the opening on its straight side, and finger-press the ear's edges before pressing them with an iron.

3. Repeat steps 1-2 to make the second ear.

4. Pin the ears to the bear's back body between the placement notches you transferred from the pattern, and baste them in place with a ³⁄₈" seam.

1. If you're using a stretchy fabric, fuse a 1"-wide strip of interfacing to the bear-front and -back hem edge to prevent distortion when you finish the hem.

2. Align and pin the front and back bear, with right sides together and the ears sandwiched between the layers. Stitch the edges with a ½" seam, pivoting at the dots just above the arms.

3. Trim the seam allowances to ¼", clipping at the curves and close to the dot at the top of the arms (be careful not to clip into your stitching) to release the arm. Finish the seam allowances and raw hem edge using your preferred method (see "Finish the seam allowances" in the Glossary on page 130).

4. Turn the bear right side out, and finger-press the edges before pressing them with an iron.

5. Fold and press the hem edge 1" toward the wrong side, and topstitch the hem with a ¾" seam.

MINI-GLOSSARY OF EMBROIDERY STITCHES

BACKSTITCH: Start by bringing your thread up from the fabric's wrong side, then take a small backward stitch through the fabric and come out a stitch length in front of the first stitch. Begin the next backstitch just ahead of where you first brought the thread up for the previous backstitch.

SATIN STITCH: Start by outlining your shape with backstitching. Then work closely spaced, straight, parallel stitches loosely across the outlined shape to completely cover it.

STEM STITCH: Work from left to right (or vice versa if you're left-handed), taking even, slightly slanted, tightly spaced stitches along the line you're embroidering. The thread should always come up slightly to the left of the end of the previous stitch.

puppet theater

I made a theater like this one for my daughter's preschool class and was amazed by the kids' reactions. All of them, even the shy and quiet ones, seemed to light up when it was their turn to be the puppeteers and when they had the chance to interact with the puppets as audience members.

The theater shown here is elaborate. All of the details shown in the photo are included in the instructions. However, it's easy to simplify this project by omitting features that don't suit you. Any finger or hand puppets (like the Bear Puppet Bath Mitt on page 109) will help to bring this theater to life.

SKILLS NEEDED

Edgestitching, Appliqué (optional), Working with large pieces of fabric

FINISHED SIZE

62" x 36" (fits doorways up to 36" wide)

MATERIALS

NOTE: In dimensions throughout, length precedes width.

1 canvas drop cloth, at least 6' x 4' (available at local hardware store) or two yds. of 44" wide canvas

FABRIC A: 2 yds. of 44"-wide quilting cotton, for house

FABRIC B: ¾ yd. of 44"-wide quilting cotton, for theater curtain

FABRIC C: 15 ½" x 8" of quilting cotton, for door

FABRIC D: ¼ yd. of 44"-wide muslin, for windows

Quilting-cotton scraps, for curtains, front step, and embellishments

Fusible appliqué web (see Resources on page 134)

7 yds. of ½"-wide ribbon or cotton twill tape, for window mullions and frames (optional)

Coordinating thread

Buttons, for embellishment (optional)

Two ½"-diameter wooden dowels, cut to 28" long

Tension shower or curtain rod, adjustable 24"-40" length

Water-soluble fabric-marking pen or chalk

Knitting needle or chopstick

Puppet Theater pattern (see Pattern Sheet 3; Pattern 15, two pieces: A-B)

PREPARE THE CANVAS

1. Cut a 67 ½" x 38" rectangle from the canvas drop cloth. Fold and press the rectangle's long, side edges to the wrong side by ½" twice, and then edgestitch the innermost fold to finish these edges.

2. Prepare the hem on the bottom edge by turning and pressing this edge twice to the wrong side, first by ½" and then by 1½". Then edgestitch the hem's innermost fold to finish it.

3. Prepare the top edge to make a casing for the curtain rod by folding and pressing it twice to the wrong side, first by ½" and then by 3". Edgestitch the casing's innermost fold to finish it.

4. On the fabric's wrong side, use a water-soluble fabric-marking pen or chalk to draw a 15" x 22" rectangle positioned as shown in the diagram below.

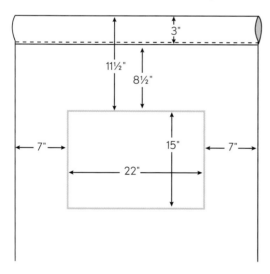

PREPARE THE HOUSE PIECES

1. In addition to the two roof pieces you cut from the pattern provided, cut pieces for the house from Fabric A as follows: one lower-house section 33½" x 30" and one upper-house section (the stage) 23" x 30". On the wrong side of the upper house (the 23" x 30" piece), mark a line 4" from each raw edge. The resulting rectangle should measure 15" x 22" and will be the stitching guide for the theater window later on.

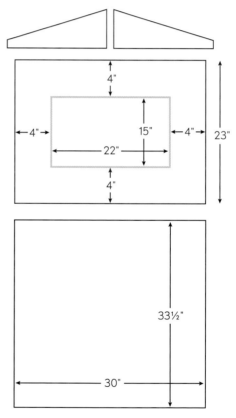

2. Align and pin the two roof pieces, with right sides facing, and stitch the longer of the two short edges (the center of the roof) with a ½" seam allowance. Press the seam allowances open, and pin the resulting long, straight edge of the roof to the top edge of the upper house, with right sides together, and join the pair with a ½" seam. Press the seam allowances open. Fold and press the raw edges of the roof to the wrong side by ½". Lay the combined upper house and roof aside temporarily.

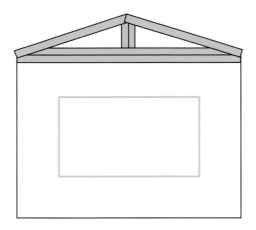

PREPARE THE DOORS AND WINDOWS

1. For the front door of the house, cut one rectangle 15 ½" x 8" wide from Fabric C. Cut two smaller pieces for the door accents, each 5 ½" square, from the quilting-cotton scraps.

2. Fold and press all the raw edges of the door and the door accents ½" to the wrong side. Then center the accent squares on the front of the door, so they are spaced 1¼" from the side edges and 2" from the top and bottom edges. Pin, and then edgestitch the accents in place.

3. For the front step, cut a rectangle 3½" x 11" from one of the quilting-cotton scraps. Fold and press the raw edges to the wrong side by ½". Then center the front step at the bottom of the lower-house panel ½" from the lower raw edge. Edgestitch the step to attach and finish it.

4. Center the door panel above the front step, so the bottom of the door touches the top edge of the step. Edgestitch the door to attach and finish it.

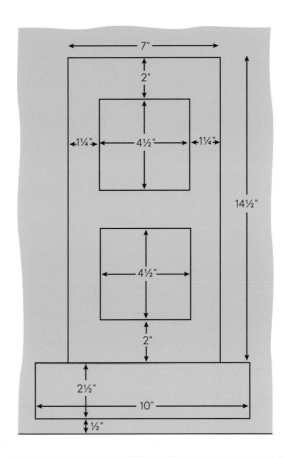

MAKE AND EMBELLISH THE WINDOWS

1. Draw five rectangles, each 9" x 6", on one of the paper liners of the fusible web. Then follow the manufacturer's directions to fuse the web to the wrong side of Fabric D for the windows.

2. Cut the fabric and the fusible web along the traced lines. Then peel the liner from the web, leaving the web on the fabric itself.

3. Position the windows on the right side of the house fabric, following the diagram at top left on page 116, and once you're happy with the placement, follow the manufacturer's directions to fuse the pieces to the house fabric.

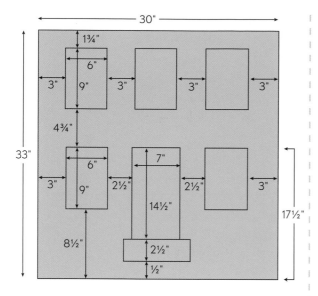

You can finish the windows very simply by just zigzag-stitching over their edges, or you can add details to the windows with additional appliqué embroidery stitches or machine-stitching. As well, you can further embellish the windows, if you want, as described in steps 4-9 below.

4. To make curtains for one window, cut a rectangle 3" x 12" from one of the quilting-cotton scraps. Hem one long edge by folding and pressing it to the wrong side by ¼" twice and then edgestitching the innermost fold to finish it. Then stitch two rows of gathering stitches ¼" and ⅜" from the other long edge, and pull on the ends of the gathering threads until the curtain is the same width as the window (6"). Pin the curtain to the top edge of one window, and baste it into position ¼" from the window's top edge. Then repeat this step to make curtains for the four remaining windows.

5. Once you have curtains and/or other embellishments in place, you can add windowpanes and frames. Start by pinning and edgestitching both sides of a 9" length of ½"-wide ribbon down the center of the window. Then pin and edgestitch both sides of a 6" length of ribbon horizontally across

the center of the window. These two ribbons will form the mullions separating the windowpanes. If necessary, trim the ends of the ribbon flush with the raw edges of the window.

6. For the window frame itself, start by pinning two 9" lengths of ½"-wide ribbon to the sides of the window. The ribbon should be positioned to cover the raw edges of the fused window rectangle. Edgestitch both sides of the ribbons to finish them.

7. For the top and bottom of the window frame, cut two 7" lengths of ribbon, and press the ends to the wrong side by ½" before pinning them to cover the raw edges of the window. Then edgestitch the ribbons, pivoting at the corners to stitch all four sides and give the window a clean finish.

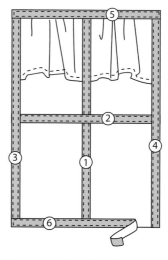

8. To add the optional window boxes, for each window box, fold and press the cut pattern piece to the wrong side along the dotted lines at the corners; then fold and press all the raw edges to the wrong side by ½". Center the window box ½" below the bottom edge of the window, and edgestitch it in place. Repeat this step for the other four window boxes.

9. Embellish the window box with appliquéd or embroidered leaves. For flowers, add appliqué, buttons, or embroidery, as desired.

10. Add any additional embellishment you want to the house, for example, some plants or bushes outside.

11. When you've finished embellishing the house, align and pin the top edge of the lower house to the bottom edge of the upper house, with right sides together. Join the pair together with a ½" seam; then press the seam allowances open.

12. Fold and press the side and bottom edges of the house to the wrong side by ½". The raw edges of the house are now all folded to the wrong side.

CREATE THE PUPPET-THEATER WINDOW, AND FINISH THE THEATER

1. Pin the right side of the house to the wrong side of the canvas so that the marked edges of the large rectangular window are aligned. Check to be sure that all the window's corners and edges match as you pin the two layers together. Then use the rectangle as a stitching guide, and pivot at the corners as you stitch all four of its sides.

2. Carefully cut through both layers of fabric in the center of the rectangle to make a hole. Then trim the fabric to approximately ¼" from your stitching line. Clip into the corners, being careful not to clip into the stitching.

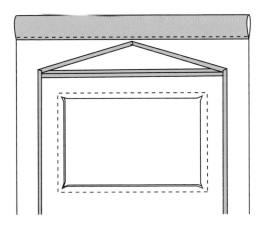

3. Turn the house to the right side of the canvas, pulling the house through the hole you've cut. Gently finger-press the rectangular window seam, rolling the seam slightly to the wrong side (the back) of the theater so that it won't show once the theater is finished. Pin through both layers of fabric near the window opening to hold them in place temporarily.

4. Lay the theater flat on the floor or a large table, so you can smooth the house against the canvas backing. Once the two layers are flat, use plenty of pins to secure them for the next steps.

5. Edgestitch the opening of the theater window to give it a clean finish.

6. With a ruler and water-soluble fabric-marking pen or chalk, draw a line extending the edgestitching at the bottom edge of the theater window to the folded side edges of the house (see the top left drawing on the next page). Draw a second line parallel to the first one, 1¼" below the first line. Then topstitch the newly drawn lines to create the casing for one of the dowels.

7. Edgestitch the perimeter of the house to the canvas to secure it, starting just above the dowel casing on one side, and stitching all the way around the perimeter of the house to stop just below the dowel casing, 1¼" below where you started. By doing this, you'll leave an opening at the end of the casing so that you can insert the dowel before stitching the opening closed.

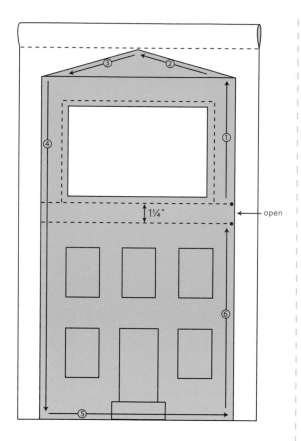

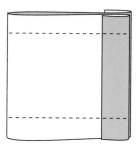

8. To help stabilize the lower part of the house, stitch the house to the canvas along the top of each window, just above the ribbon. This will prevent the house fabric from separating and possibly sagging once you hang the theater.

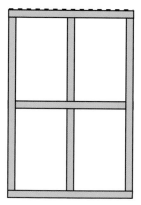

1. To make casing holders for a curtain rod, cut two rectangles from a leftover scrap of lightweight fabric (you might use the same fabric you selected for the curtain), each 2" x 5". Fold the short ends of one rectangle to the wrong side by ½", and press them. Then fold the rectangle in half, with right sides together and the short ends matching. Stitch the sides with a ¼" seam; then turn the resulting rectangle right side out through the open (folded) short end. Use a knitting needle or chopstick to gently push out the corners; then press the casing with an iron. Prepare the second casing the same way.

2. On the back of the theater, pin the casing rectangles at opposite corners of the house, ¾" below the outer edge of the roof-line stitching and flush with the sides of the house (use your edgestitching line as a guide). Position the unstitched end of the casing toward the outside; then edgestitch the three outside edges of the rectangles to the theater, making sure to change your bobbin thread to match the color of the house. The edgestitching will close up the opening in the casing. Alternatively you can blindstitch the outside edges of the rectangles to the canvas by hand, so the stitches don't show on the front of the theater.

118

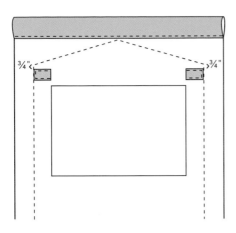

MAKE THE CURTAIN

1. Cut a 23" length of Fabric B using the full width of the fabric. Fold the fabric in half, widthwise, matching the selvedges, and crease the resulting fold. Then cut the fabric in half on the crease to make two equal rectangles 23" x 22".

2. Fold and press the side edges of each rectangle to the wrong side by ¼" twice, and edgestitch the innermost fold to finish the sides of the curtains.

3. Hem the bottom edge of each curtain by turning and pressing it twice to the wrong side by ½", and edgestitch the innermost fold.

4. Prepare the top edge for the dowel/curtain rod by folding and pressing it twice to the wrong side, first by ½", and then by 1". Edgestitch the innermost fold on each curtain to finish the curtain-rod casing.

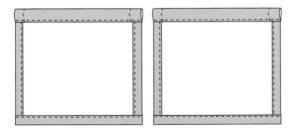

FINISH THE THEATER

1. Insert one ½"-diameter dowel into the casing below the theater window on the front of the curtain. Then hand-stitch the casing opening closed with a blindstitch.

2. Stitch a button to the front door for a door handle.

3. Feed the curtain casings onto the second ½"-diameter dowel, and insert the ends of the dowel into the casings above the theater window.

4. Insert the tension rod into the casing at the top of the puppet theater. The tension rod can be adjusted to fit a variety of door widths as needed.

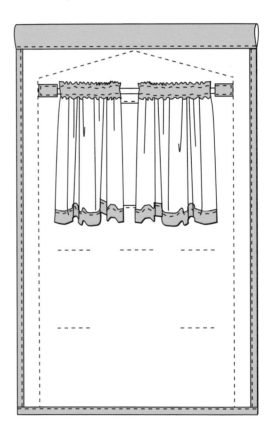

appendix

oliver + s basic techniques

MEASUREMENT AND CUTTING INSTRUCTIONS

All projects with sizes are based on the following body measurements, which will be helpful to have on hand when determining what size to make.

SIZE	CHEST	WAIST	HIP	HEIGHT	WEIGHT
6-12 M	19"	19½"	19½"	27-29"	17-22 LBS
12-18 M	19¾"	20½"	20½"	29-31"	22-27 LBS
18-24 M	20½"	21"	21"	31-33"	27-30 LBS
2T	21"	21"	22"	33-36"	30-33 LBS
3T	21½"	21"	23"	36-39"	33-36 LBS
4	22½"	21½"	24"	39-42"	36-39 LBS
5	23½"	22"	25½"	42-45"	39-44 LBS
6	24½"	22½"	26½"	45-49"	45-55 LBS
7	25½"	23"	27½"	49-52"	56-64 LBS
8	26½"	23½"	28½"	52-54"	65-72 LBS
10	28"	24"	30"	54-56"	73-77 LBS

To help you understand what the measurements on this chart mean, use the guidelines at right. Note, too, that some of these garment projects include measurements for several sizes, with the smallest size given first and the larger sizes following immediately in parentheses—for example, in the Explorer's Vest (page 98): *Small*, fits up to size 3 (*medium*, sizes 4-6; *large*, sizes 7-10); chest, 25 ½" (28 ½", 30 ½"); and length from shoulder seam at neckline, 13 ¾" (16 ¼", 18 ⅝").

LENGTH FROM SHOULDER SEAM AT NECKLINE: Measured from the highest part of the shoulder line—where the shoulder seam meets the neckline—to the hem of the garment.

SLEEVE LENGTH FROM CENTER BACK: Measured from the center back of the garment at the neckline, across to the shoulder, and then down the sleeve to the sleeve hem.

CHEST: The chest's circumference measured just below the arms.

1. Read all instructions carefully before you begin.

2. Wash, dry, and iron your fabric and any trims before starting.

3. When making a garment, for best fit, measure the child's chest, waist, hip, and height to determine the correct size before cutting.

4. Note that seam allowances are included in the patterns and are ½" unless otherwise noted.

5. When sewing, always press your seams as you progress through construction: First set the seams by pressing them flat; then press the seam allowances open unless otherwise instructed.

6. After stitching, clip the seam allowances where necessary to help the seams lie flat, especially at curves or where multiple layers are joined.

TRACING A PATTERN

In order to preserve the original pattern sheets included with this book, we suggest that you trace each pattern on a separate sheet of paper, and cut out the traced pattern, instead of cutting into the original. To do this, you'll need tracing paper and a sharp pencil. Some people like to use tissue paper, but I prefer to purchase lightweight tracing paper on a roll, which will last for many projects.

1. Lay the tracing paper on top of the pattern you want to trace, and weight or tape both the pattern sheet and tracing paper to prevent them from shifting.

2. Use your pencil to copy all the lines and markings of the pattern on the tracing paper. You may find it helpful to identify the lines you want to trace by drawing over them on the pattern sheet with a highlighter before you begin tracing.

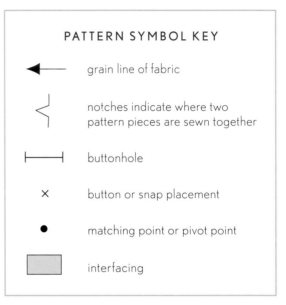

ILLUSTRATION KEY

right side   wrong side   lining   interfacing

PATTERN SYMBOL KEY

← grain line of fabric

notches indicate where two pattern pieces are sewn together

⊢—⊣ buttonhole

× button or snap placement

● matching point or pivot point

interfacing

TIPS FOR PATTERN AND FABRIC LAYOUT AND CUTTING

1. Follow the cutting directions on each pattern piece, cutting the piece in the number and fabrics called for.

2. If the instructions call for cutting a pattern piece twice and you're using a single layer of fabric, remember to flip the pattern piece over before cutting it a second time so that you'll have cut a mirror-image pattern piece.

3. A handful of patterns in the book have suggested layout guides (see page 124) to help you position the pattern pieces most efficiently on the fabric before cutting. Note that the layout guides show positioning of the pattern pieces for the largest size and that, if you're using a smaller size, the pieces may fit together more closely than those shown.

4. Whenever cutting out patterns, pin or weight the pattern pieces on the fabric to prevent them from shifting while you cut.

5. Cut accurately along the outside of the pattern lines, using very sharp scissors or a rotary cutter (and cutting mat).

6. Transfer the pattern markings to the side of the fabric indicated in the directions, using chalk or a water-soluble fabric-marking pen that washes out. See the Pattern Symbol Key on page 122 for an explanation of the markings and "Transfer markings from the pattern to the fabric" below for detailed how-to information.

7. As a general rule of thumb, to eliminate confusion later, if the fabric you're using looks the same on both sides, be sure to mark the side you designate as the wrong side with chalk or a water-soluble fabric-marking pen, and leave the pattern pieces pinned to the cut fabric until you're ready to use them.

TRANSFERING MARKINGS FROM THE PATTERN TO THE FABRIC

1. Use a water-soluble fabric-marking pen, chalk, or a tracing wheel and carbon paper to transfer all the markings from your pattern to the fabric. Markings are usually transferred to the wrong side of the cut fabric, but the instructions will tell you if they should instead be transferred to the fabric's right side. If you cut two layers of fabric at the same time, be sure to mark both layers.

2. With the pattern piece still pinned to the cut fabric piece(s), transfer the markings with chalk or a water-soluble fabric-marking pen as follows: Starting at the pattern piece's outside edge and working into the center, use a straight pin to poke through each pattern marking that needs transferring, and mark the pin's position on the fabric's wrong side (or right side, depending on the project instructions) with the chalk or fabric-marking pen. If you're marking two layers of cut fabric, separate the layers just enough to mark the pin's location on both layers. If the pattern marking is more than a single point, pull the pin out after marking its first position, move it over a little on the pattern marking, poke through the pattern marking again, and mark the pin's new position on the fabric. Continue like this until you've transferred the entire pattern marking.

3. To transfer a pattern marking with a tracing wheel and carbon paper, first select the lightest carbon color that will show up on your fabric since you may not be able to remove the carbon markings. Also, if you're using a tracing wheel with a serrated edge, be sure to protect your work surface by using a cutting mat under the pattern. Then, with the carbon paper carbon side up, place the fabric's wrong side on top of it, and the traced pattern on top of the fabric; and use the tracing wheel to follow and transfer the pattern markings, pressing firmly so that the carbon transfers to the fabric.

If you have two layers of fabric, remove the pattern piece and place the unmarked side onto the carbon paper and use the tracing wheel to follow the transferred markings onto the other side.

FABRIC LAYOUT AND CUTTING DIAGRAMS

Use these layout and cutting diagrams to help position the pattern pieces on your fabric in the most efficient way possible. If a layout shows a piece extending past the fabric's fold, cut out all the pattern pieces except that piece. Then open up the remaining fabric flat, single-layer, and right side up; and cut the full pattern piece with its extending section as indicated.

SMALL MESSENGER BAG

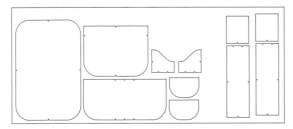

Fabric A

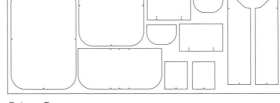

Fabric B

LARGE MESSENGER BAG

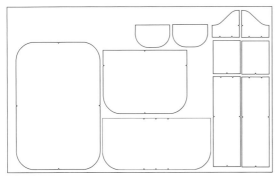

Fabric A

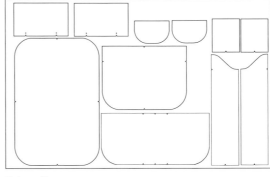

Fabric B

PENGUIN BACKPACK

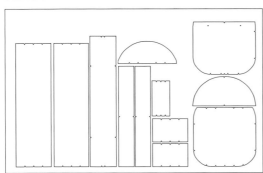

Fabric A

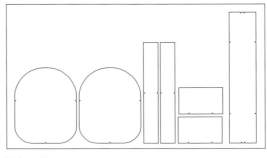

Fabric B

BIAS-TRIMMED
APRON

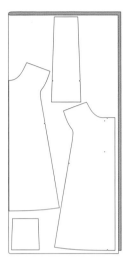

ART SMOCK

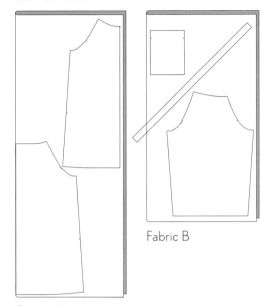

Fabric B

Fabric A

RED RIDING HOOD

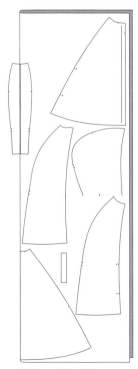

Fabrics A + B

EXPLORER VEST

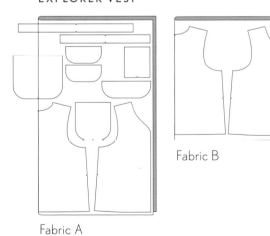

Fabric A

Fabric B

KEY

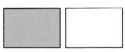

right side   wrong side

WORKING WITH BIAS BINDING

Bias binding offers a simple, practical way to finish the edges of many items. It can eliminate the need for facings, linings, and hems on apparel and makes a neat edge on quilts, bags, and many other sewing projects.

READY-MADE VS. HANDMADE BINDING

You can buy packages of ready-made bias binding in a wide variety of colors and widths, or you can make your own bias binding, using your choice of fabric. I prefer to make my own, so I can customize it to my project, using printed fabrics or a particular color that may not be easily available in a ready-made binding (also I prefer to use 100% cotton fabric, and most ready-made bias binding uses a poly/cotton blend that just doesn't look or feel as nice).

If you use a bias tape maker (see Resources on page 134), you'll find it quick and fun to make your own bias binding. You can still make bias binding even if you don't own a bias tape maker (although it takes a little more time). There are several ways to make bias binding and apply it (whether homemade or ready-made) to an edge, and my favorite method is described below.

CUTTING AND JOINING BIAS STRIPS

Plain-woven fabric is made from a series of lengthwise threads interwoven with one or more crosswise threads. The fabric's grain runs both lengthwise (where it's called the straight grain) and crosswise (where it's called the cross grain). The fabric's "true" bias runs at a 45-degree angle to its straight and cross grains, and fabric cut on the bias is stretchy and conforms nicely to a curve. For these reasons,

bias-cut strips are excellent for binding and finishing the raw edges of many projects.

1. To cut your own bias, start by laying your fabric opened out flat, single-layer, and wrong side up. Check to be sure the fabric's grain lines are straight, and trim the edges if necessary to square up the fabric. Use a fabric-marking pen or chalk to draw a line ¼" from the top and bottom edges of the fabric (these lines will serve as your seam lines when you join the strips together after cutting them). Fold the fabric diagonally so that the lengthwise grain aligns with the crosswise grain. Press and then cut along this diagonal fold, which will produce a bias cut. You can then mark lines parallel to this cut edge to make bias strips at whatever width you need.

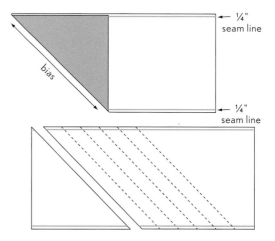

2. To determine the width of the binding strips you'll need, multiply the finished binding width that you want by 4. For example, for a ⅜"-wide finished binding, you'll need to start with 1½"-wide bias strips, while a ½"-wide finished binding requires starting with 2"-wide bias strips.

3. Cut as many bias strips as you think you'll need for the length of the edge to be bound, and then join the strips as follows: Pin the ends of two strips together at one of the seam lines you drew, with the fabric's right sides together and at a 90-degree angle to one another, as shown in the illustration.

4. Then stitch along the seam line, and press the seam open. Trim off any points that extend beyond the strip. Continue to join the strips this way until you have enough for your project.

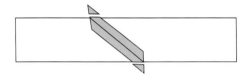

FOLDING AND PRESSING BIAS BINDING

1. If you have a bias-strip maker, follow the manufacturer's instructions to feed the joined bias strips though the larger of the tool's two openings, and press the folded strip as it emerges from the other end of the strip maker. Then fold and press the strip in half along its length so that the bias strip's raw edges are completely enclosed. Your bias strip is finished and ready to apply to your project.

2. If you don't have a special bias strip maker to help with preparing the joined bias strip, simply fold the strip in half along its length, with wrong sides together; and press a crease into the fold. Then open up the folded strip, and fold and press each of the strip's long raw edges toward the center crease.

Finish preparing the bias strip by refolding and pressing it at the center crease to completely enclose the raw edges inside the folds. Try not to stretch the bias strip as you're folding and pressing it since that will narrow the width of the finished bias strip.

APPLYING BIAS BINDING

There are two simple steps to my favorite method of applying bias binding:

1. Unfold the prepared bias strip, and align and pin the right side of one of its raw edges to the inside (wrong-side) edge of your project. Stitch the bias strip to the fabric in the first crease of the bias strip.

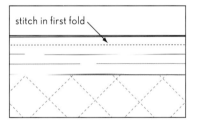

stitch in first fold

2. Re-fold the strip around the edge of the project, and turn your project to the right side (the outside). Then edgestitch the bias strip's folded edge to the right side of the fabric, so it covers the first stitching line. This method gives a nice, clean finish to the tape on both sides of your project.

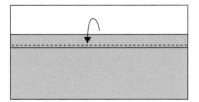

FINISHING THE ENDS OF AN APPLIED BIAS STRIP

If you're applying bias binding to only one edge and need to finish the strip's ends neatly, here's how to do it:

1. In your first pass of stitching (Step 1 of "Applying bias binding" on page 127), pin and stitch the un-folded bias strip so that it extends beyond the edge to which it is being applied. Then trim the end of the binding to extend only about ¼" beyond that edge.

2. Trim the corner seam allowance of the edge itself at a slight diagonal to reduce bulk, and fold the trimmed end of the bias strip over that edge to the right side. Re-fold the long edge of the bias strip around the edge being covered, and edgestitch the bias strip from the right side (Step 2 of "Applying bias binding" on page 127), catching the folded edge of the bias in your stitching, and backstitching or lockstitching at the beginning and end of your stitches to secure them.

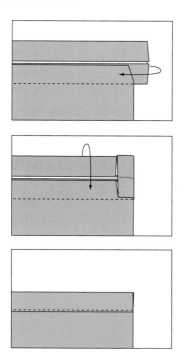

JOINING THE TWO ENDS

When you need to join two ends of a continuous bias strip, here is an easy way to clean-finish that join:

Fold and press one short end of the bias strip ½" to the wrong side before you begin stitching that first end of the strip to the project's edge. After stitching the first edge, trim the second end so that it overlaps the first end and the two raw edges end at the same spot. Then re-fold the bias strip, and edgestitch its second folded edge from the right side of the project to finish the binding, or blindstitch in place for a perfect finish. The join will be a nearly invisible fold.

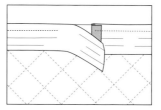

BIAS HINTS

To prepare bias binding for a curved edge (like the armholes on the Explorer Vest on page 98), fold and steam-press the folded binding into a curve as you prepare it. This will help the binding conform to the curved edge and make it easier to apply.

To attach bias binding to a thick fabric, like a quilt or heavy wool, stitch the first seam of the binding a little narrower than the first folded crease. The little bit of extra fabric this provides will enable the binding to comfortably wrap around the thickness of the quilt or fabric and reach the other side.

GLOSSARY

APPLIQUÉ: A piece of fabric sewn either by hand or machine to a larger piece of fabric, often for embellishment. When attaching an appliqué by machine, we suggest using a satin stitch. (See *Satin stitch*.)

BACKSTITCH: Backstitching can be sewn by machine or hand, and the purpose of each stitch is very different. Backstitching by machine involves sewing a few stitches in reverse at the beginning or end of a seam to anchor the seam and prevent the stitches from coming unsewn. Backstitching by hand is a decorative stitch often used to outline an area (see page 111 for a drawing and how-to information).

BARTACK: Closely set zigzag stitches sewn to reinforce areas of a garment or project subject to stress, such as pocket openings or buttonholes.

BASTING STITCH: Long stitches, frequently used to hold multiple layers of fabric together or in position temporarily during construction, which can be easily removed later. Basting can be done by machine (by simply setting the machine to its longest stitch length) or by hand (usually with a long running stitch). (See also *Running stitch*.)

BATTING: The middle layer of a quilt sandwich, usually made of cotton or wool fibers that have been processed and wadded or "flattened" into loose rolls or sheets. Batting can be purchased in a variety of sizes and thicknesses, or lofts (see Resources on page 134).

BIAS: Any straight line that doesn't run directly on the fabric's straight or cross grain is referred to as being on the bias or off-grain. Fabric cut on the bias has more stretch and drape than fabric cut on the straight or cross grain, but bias cuts can distort or twist much more easily than straight- or cross-grain cuts. (See also *Bias binding*, *Grain*, *True bias*, and "Working with bias binding" on page 126.)

BIAS BINDING: A narrow strip of fabric cut on the bias that's frequently used to encase a raw edge of a project or another fabric. Ready-made bias binding can be can be bought in packages, or you can make your own bias binding, speeding up the process with a handy tool called a bias tape maker (see "Working with bias binding" on page 126). (See also *Bias*.)

BINDING: A narrow strip of fabric, whether cut as a straight-grain strip or a bias strip, that's used to encase the raw edge of a quilt or other fabric. (See also *Bias binding*.)

BLINDSTITCH: A hand stitch used to join two edges (for example, a hem to a garment) almost invisibly. Sew a blindstitch as follows, using a single strand of knotted thread in a hand needle: Working from right to left with your needle pointing to the left (or vice versa if you're left-handed) and keeping your stitches loose and very small, roll the folded fabric edge back about ¼", and take a tiny stitch in this edge. Then take a tiny stitch in the main fabric about ³⁄₈" to the left of the first stitch (picking up only a couple of threads on the back of the fabric to keep the stitch from showing on the right side). Take another very small stitch in the folded edge ³⁄₈" to the left, and continue alternating stitching between the folded edge and garment fabric, producing a series of small "V's."

CASING: A narrow channel of fabric often used to hold elastic or a drawstring in place.

DRAPE: The term drape refers to the way a fabric folds or hangs on the body when worn. A fabric with good drape will form soft, natural folds, while a fabric with poor drape will stand away stiffly from the body. Note that some designs call for fabric with fluid drape, while other more structured designs require stiffer fabric with little drape.

EASE: Easing involves machine-sewing gathering or basting stitches on a longer edge (often a sleeve cap) that needs to fit to a shorter edge (in the case of a sleeve cap, the armhole). By gently pulling the stitches' thread tails, you can draw in and narrow the longer edge without actually gathering it and thus ease it to fit the shorter edge to which it's to be sewn. Easing produces volume in the area eased and, in the case of a sleeve cap, allows the cap to fit the curve of the shoulder. (See also *Basting stitch* and *Gathering stitch*.)

EDGESTITCH: A straight stitch sewn from the right side of the fabric that's between $1/16$" or $1/8$" from and parallel to a fabric's edge, a seam, or another stitching line, which anchors, reinforces, or finishes that edge, seam, or stitching line. When edgestitching, use the edge of your presser foot as a stitching guide. (See also *Topstitch*.)

FAT QUARTER: Often used in quilting, a fat quarter is $1/4$ yard of fabric (usually a quilting cotton), cut to measure 18" wide x 22" long instead of the typical 9"-wide x 42"-long $1/4$-yard cut.

FEED DOGS: The grooved "teeth" on a sewing machine bed directly below the presser foot that hold the fabric against the presser foot while stitches are being formed and also move the fabric through the machine as it stitches.

FINGER-PRESS: As its name suggests, finger-pressing involves folding an edge or crease in the fabric or folding open a seam's allowances by running your finger or thumbnail several times over the fold, crease, or opened allowances to "press" them. Sometimes after finger-pressing, project directions will call for additionally pressing the fabric with an iron, in which case the finger-pressing will improve the accuracy of the iron pressing.

FINISH THE SEAM ALLOWANCES: You can finish the raw edges on seam allowances several different ways. We suggest zigzag-stitching each seam allowance's raw edge, straight-stitching $1/4$" from the raw edge, or trimming the edge with pinking shears to prevent raveling. You can also finish seam allowances with a serger. Note, too, that some directions tell you to press the seam allowances together to one side (instead of pressing them open), and, in this case, you can finish the seam allowances together as one unit. (See also *Seam allowance*.)

FOLD LINE: Pattern pieces are often cut on the fold to make a single cut-fabric pattern piece without a center seam. When positioning a pattern piece to be cut on the fold, make sure to place the edge marked "Cut on fold" on the fabric's fold, which should run parallel to the fabric's grain.

FUSE: Using the heat of the iron to melt a glue adhesive on a fabric. Fusible web, which is often used for appliqué, is made of a dry glue adhesive that melts when heated to adhere two fabrics together. A dry adhesive is also applied to fusible interfacings, which enables the interfacing to stick to the back of the fabric to which it is being applied.

GATHERING STITCH: A long straight stitch (when sewn on a machine) or running stitch (when sewn by hand) that's used to cinch, or gather in, and shorten a length of fabric. To gather by machine, loosen your machine tension slightly so that the bobbin thread can be pulled easily. Then stitch ³⁄₈" from the raw edge of the fabric across the length being gathered. Stitch a second row of gathering stitches ⁵⁄₈" from the raw edge, leaving long thread tails at the beginning and end of each row of stitches. Next, pull the bobbin-thread tails on each row to gather the stitched fabric, adjusting the fullness evenly across the gathered area. Once you've basted and sewn the gathered area to the garment, remove the two rows of gathering stitches.

GRAIN: The term grain refers to the direction in which the yarns, or threads, are woven in a fabric. The fabric's grain runs both lengthwise (parallel to the selvedges) and widthwise (perpendicular to the selvedges). The lengthwise grain (or warp) is called the straight grain, while the widthwise grain (or weft) is called the cross grain. (See also *Bias*.)

HEM: The finished edge of a garment (usually the bottom edge), often formed by folding under and pressing the raw edge twice before topstitching the innermost fold. A hem can also be sewn by hand with a blindstitch. (See also *Blindstitch*.)

INTERFACING: A special layer of fabric that adds shape and stability to another fabric (often in a facing, placket, or collar) and prevents that fabric from stretching or distorting. Interfacing can be a woven or nonwoven fabric and, depending on its makeup, is sewn or fused to the fabric. Select interfacings carefully to complement the fabric and the project for which they'll be used.

LOCKSTITCH: An easy, almost invisible stitching technique used to secure the stitches at the beginning and end of a stitching line. To lockstitch, position your fabric under the needle at the beginning of the stitching line, and set the machine's stitch length to zero (or the lowest stitch length your machine offers); then take a couple of stitches in place. Reset the stitch length to its regular stitching length, and sew the stitching line. At the end of the stitching line, reset the stitch length to zero or the shortest length possible, and take a couple of stitches in place.

NOTCH: A triangular marking at a pattern piece's edge that's cut away when the fabric pattern piece is cut. The notched edge is then used to help assemble the pattern correctly by matching similarly notched fabric edges to be sewn together.

PIVOT: Pivoting involves changing stitching direction at a corner or another angled point in the stitching line. To pivot, stop with the needle down in the fabric when you arrive at the pivot point, and lift the presser foot. Then rotate, or pivot, the fabric to the new stitching position, lower the presser foot, and continue stitching.

PRESS THE SEAM ALLOWANCES: After sewing a seam, press the seam flat to set it. Then, depending on the project directions, you can either press the seam allowances open (away from the seam line) or together to one side.

RIGHT SIDE: The side of the fabric that will be visible when the project is finished. On some fabrics, there is no discernable right side, so you can designate either side as the right side.

RUNNING STITCH: A simple hand-sewing stitch in which the needle and thread move in and out of the fabric, with the stitches and spaces between them consistently about ⅛" long. When you elongate the running stitch to about ¼" in length, it becomes a hand-basting stitch. (See also *Basting stitch*.)

SATIN STITCH: Satin stitches can be sewn by machine or by hand. On a machine, the smooth texture of satin stitching is created by sewing closely set zigzag stitches, which are often used to finish a fabric's raw edge or to machine-appliqué one fabric onto another. A satin stitch sewn by hand (see page 111 for a drawing and how-to information) is generally used for embellishment.

SEAM ALLOWANCE: The fabric between a seam's stitching line and the fabric's cut edge make up the seam allowance. All Oliver + S patterns, including those in this book, have a ½" seam allowance built into them (unless the project directions state a different width), and therefore seam allowances do not need to be added to the patterns. (See also *Finish the seam allowances*, *Press the seam allowances*, and *Trim the seam allowances*.)

SELVEDGE (OR SELVAGE): The narrow finished lengthwise edges of a woven fabric, usually ¼" to ½" wide, that are often more tightly woven than the rest of the fabric (which prevents the fabric from tearing when it is finished at the mill). Because the selvedges are constructed differently than the rest of the fabric, they may shrink at a different rate than the rest of the fabric when washed. Selvedges should generally be removed before sewing.

STAYSTITCH: A row of straight stitching within a cut-fabric pattern piece's seam allowance that helps stabilize an edge like an armhole or neck edge to keep it from stretching or distorting during construction. Staystitching is usually sewn on a single layer of fabric ⅛" from the seam line, so it won't show after construction. For most Oliver + S patterns, including those in this book, staystitching is done ⅜" from the fabric's edge.

STEM STITCH: A hand-embroidery stitch often used to outline an area (see page 111 for a drawing and how-to information).

TACKING: Hand-sewing several small stitches in one spot or area to discretely secure one fabric or element to another (like a folded-back sleeve cuff tacked in place).

TOPSTITCH: Straight-stitching sewn from the right side and more than ⅛" (and up to several inches or more) from and parallel to an edge, seam, or another stitching line. Edgestitching and topstitching are essentially the same thing, with the only difference between them being the distance from the edge, seam, or other stitching line. (See also *Edgestitch*.)

TRIM THE SEAM ALLOWANCES: Trimming the seam allowances (the fabric that runs from the seam line to the fabric's raw edge) reduces a seam's bulk so that when you press the seam or edge from the right side, you'll get nice, crisp results. Trim seam allowances with scissors (not a rotary cutter) to about ⅛" (but no less) in width. Also take care to follow any directions that explicitly say not to trim the seam allowances at a certain point, for example, along an opening left for turning the work right side out. (See also *Seam allowance*.)

TRUE BIAS: A 45-degree angle to the warp and weft threads. Fabric cut on the true bias has lots of stretch and drape and conforms nicely to contours. (See also **Bias binding**, **Grain**, and "Working with bias binding" on page 126.)

UNDERSTITCH: Understitching helps keep the facing/lining seam and the facing/lining itself inside the garment and prevents them from showing when the garment is worn. To understitch, press the facing or lining away from the garment, and press the seam allowances toward the facing/lining. With the facing side up, edgestitch close to the seam, sewing through the facing/lining and the seam allowances.

WALKING FOOT: A special foot attachment for the sewing machine that feeds fabric layers through the machine evenly. A walking foot is commonly used for quilting, but it can also be very helpful for sewing thick layers of fabric or fabrics that might stick to the sewing machine bed.

WARP: The yarns in a fabric that run parallel to the selvedge are called the warp. These are the fabric's foundation yarns and are wound onto the loom before the fabric is woven. Warp yarns are usually the strongest yarns. Your fabric will drape nicely if you cut and sew so that the warp hangs perpendicular to the floor when the garment is finished. (See also **Grain**.)

WEFT: The yarns that run across the fabric, from selvedge to selvedge. These are the secondary yarns of the fabric, or the fill yarns. These yarns are not as strong as the warp yarns and often have a little stretch or give in them, even when a fabric is not a stretch fabric. (See also **Grain**.)

WRONG SIDE: The side of the fabric that will not be visible when finished. On printed fabrics, the wrong side is the one without the design. On some fabrics, there is no discernable right or wrong side—both look the same—and you can designate either side as the wrong (or right) side. (See also Tip 7 in "Tips for pattern and fabric layout and cutting" on page 122.)

ZIGZAG STITCH: A straight machine stitch that changes directions with each stitch, creating a zigzag effect. Zigzag stitches are frequently used to finish seam allowances, but they can also be used for decorative stitching. Zigzag stitches set very close together can also be used for bartacking or for satin stitching. (See also **Bartack** and **Satin stitch**.)

resources

RECOMMENDED SUPPLIES

Every seamstress has her favorite products. I'm no exception. Below are some of my favorite manufacturers of supplies I used to complete the projects in this book. Contact your local retailer or favorite online stores to see if they carry these products.

BIAS TAPE MAKER: Clover Needlecraft (www.clover-usa.com)

CUSTOM-PRINTED FABRICS: Spoonflower (www.spoonflower.com)

COTTON STUFFING: Quilter's Dream Sweet Dreams Stuffing (www.quiltersdreambatting.com) and Fairfield Nature-fil (www.poly-fil.com)

FUSIBLE APPLIQUÉ WEB: Mistyfuse (www.mistyfuse.com) and HeatnBond Lite (www.thermowebonline.com)

INTERFACING, LIGHTWEIGHT FUSIBLE: HeatnBond Feather Weight Iron-On Fusible (www.thermowebonline.com)

IRON-ON VINYL: HeatnBond Iron-On Vinyl in matte finish (www.thermowebonline.com)

QUILT BATTING: Quilter's Dream (www.quiltersdream.com)

TEMPLATE PLASTIC: Collins rigid vinyl template plastic sheets (www.dritz.com)

THREAD: Gutermann (www.gutermann-thread.com)

TRACING PAPER: Canson canary sketch/tracing paper (www.canson-us.com) and Pellon Easy Pattern (www.pellonideas.com)

WOOL FABRICS: Mary Flanagan Woolens (www.mfwoolens.com) and Weeks Dye Works (www.weeksdyeworks.com)

SPECIALTY SUPPLIES

Some of the harder-to-come-by supplies required for projects can be purchased online from the following specialty retailers if you can't find them locally.

CARBON PAPER: Pacific Trimming (www.pacifictrimming.com) and Steinlauf and Stoller (www.steinlaufandstoller.com)

LINEN FABRICS: Grayline Linen (www.graylinelinen.com)

RIBBON AND TWILL TAPE: M&J Trimming (www.mjtrim.com), Tinsel Trading (www.tinseltrading.com), and Pacific Trimming (www.pacifictrimming.com)

STRAP ADJUSTERS: Pacific Trimming (www.pacifictrimming.com)

TRACING WHEEL: Pacific Trimming (www.pacifictrimming.com) and Steinlauf and Stoller (www.steinlaufandstoller.com)

VELCRO, COLORED (HOOK-AND-LOOP TAPE): Pacific Trimming (www.pacifictrimming.com)

recommended reading

Several of my favorite sewing books are out of print. These titles (marked with an asterisk below) can still be found in used bookstores and thrift stores, and on the internet.

* Bishop, Edna Bryte, and Marjorie Stotler Arch. *The Bishop Method of Clothing Construction.* Revised Edition. Philadelphia: J.B. Lippincott Company, 1966.

The gold standard of apparel sewing books, this is an excellent resource for learning to sew as well as for improving your skills and knowledge. I highly recommend this book for anyone's collection. I prefer the 1966 edition because it includes a section on "torn projects" that teaches you how to sew basic garments like a skirt and an apron without using a pattern.

Hoverson, Joelle. *Last-Minute Patchwork + Quilted Gifts.* New York: Stewart, Tabori & Chang, 2007.

This book offers a great deal of information and inspiration about quilts and quilt-making. The materials section in the back is also thorough and very useful.

* Kittleson, Christine, ed. *The New Sewing Essentials (Singer Sewing Reference Library).* Minnetonka, MN: Creative Publishing International, 1998.

This was my first sewing book, and it gives an excellent introduction to apparel sewing as well as to working with a sewing pattern. It's a wonderful book to refer to as your skills progress, as well.

* *McCall's New Complete Book of Sewing and Dressmaking.* Revised Edition. New York: Greystone Press, 1957.

Although this book is intended for sewing women's apparel, the techniques are excellent and the instructions are very thorough. Ignore the somewhat kitschy text ("Have you your shoulder pads?"), and focus instead on the technical content. This book will help you improve your sewing to achieve professional-looking results. I love the photos!

Singer, Ruth. *The Sewing Bible: A Modern Manual of Practical and Decorative Sewing Techniques.* New York: Potter Craft, 2009.

I appreciate this book because, like the Bishop Method book, it starts out with the basics and builds gradually without throwing a beginner into using patterns right away. It's also an excellent reference book.

acknowledgments

First of all, thanks to all our Oliver + S customers, many of whom have also become friends. Your enthusiasm and valuable feedback inspire me daily.

Thanks to Melanie Falick, my editor, who understood the Oliver + S brand and gave me the creative freedom to produce the type of book I wanted. She also made it possible for me to use the talents of the same great team of people who work on our sewing patterns.

Thanks go to everyone on our team: to Brooke Hellewell Reynolds, my dear friend and our visual designer; to Chris Timmons, our astute technical editor who ensures the clarity of our instructions; to Dan Andreasen, who illustrates our paper dolls; and to Adrienne Bockheim, who is both our lightning-quick technical illustrator and my sister.

I'm also grateful to the group of very talented seamstresses who tested all the projects in the book and sewed most of the items appearing in the photographs: Beth Bacher, Julie Bockheim, April Henry, JoLyn Knight, Karen Knight, Meg Lineberger, Jeanne Po, and Sandy Stewart.

We were fortunate to find almost all the models for the photographs right in our neighborhood. Many of them are also our friends. Thanks to Audrey, Bibi, Cirène, Eleanor, Jasper, Leilani, Lino, Logan, Londyn, Matthew, Makinlee, Maxie, Mosiah, Mia, Michelle, Oscar, Olivia, Ranan, and S, as well as to all their parents. Models provided some of their own clothing and additional wardrobe was provided by Tea (www.teacollection.com) and Oliver + S.

The photography team for the book was a pleasure to work with. Thanks to Laurie Frankel, Diane Gatterdam, Richard Rose, and Markus Kingsley.

Many of the fabrics you see in the book are my own designs. I am grateful to Stephen Fraser and Danielle Hazen at Spoonflower (www.spoonflower.com) who worked with me to match the colors and provided me with the yardage needed to make samples. What better way to create a truly unique little item than to make it with fabric you designed and had printed by Spoonflower? Other fabrics were graciously provided by the following manufacturers: Michael Miller, P&B Textiles, Robert Kaufman, and Weeks Dye Works.

The Travel Quilt was designed using Electric Quilt 6 software provided by The Electric Quilt Company.

My friends Heather Ross and Claudia Albuquerque offered me support and provided excellent feedback while I was writing this book.

I owe a very special thanks to Giulia Tissi, who worked with me for several months as I completed the book, helping me write and troubleshoot the patterns and test many of the projects. This book is truly a better product thanks to her involvement.

And finally, thanks to my husband, Todd, our daughter, S (my inspiration!), and to my family—especially my mom and my grandma. I love you all!

BASE 1

BASE 1

BASE 2

BASE 2

PAPER DOLLS

To play with these Oliver + S paper dolls, first remove this page from the book along the perforated line, then cut out each doll and base. Insert Base 1 into Base 2 to make your doll stand. To dress the dolls, carefully cut out the clothing on this book's jacket.